CURR 470 R552e

D1038739

EASY LATIN CROSSWORD PUZZLES

QUID PRO QUO

BETTY WALLACE ROBINETT
VIRGINIA FRENCH ALLEN

EDUCATION CURRICULUM VF

PASSPORT BOOKS
NTC/Contemporary Publishing Group

BUSWELL MEMORIAL LIBRARY
WHEATON COLLEGE
WHEATON, IL 60187

Other titles in this series:

Easy French Crossword Puzzles
Easy German Crossword Puzzles
Easy Italian Crossword Puzzles
Easy Japanese Crossword Puzzles Using Kana
Easy Japanese Crossword Puzzles Using Roomaji
Easy Spanish Crossword Puzzles

Cover design by Kim Bartko
Cover illustration copyright © Mark Anderson

Published by Passport Books
A division of NTC/Contemporary Publishing Group, Inc.
4255 West Touhy Avenue, Lincolnwood (Chicago), Illinois 60712-1975 U.S.A.
Copyright © 1999 by NTC/Contemporary Publishing Group, Inc.
All rights reserved. No part of this book may be reproduced, stored in a retrieval
system, or transmitted in any form or by any means, electronic, mechanical,
photocopying, recording, or otherwise, without the prior written permission of
NTC/Contemporary Publishing Group, Inc.
Printed in the United States of America
International Standard Book Number: 0-8442-8446-7
Library of Congress Catalog Card Number: 99-70527
00 01 02 03 04 05 VP 20 19 18 17 16 15 14 13 12 11 10 9 8 7 6 5 4 3 2

Contents

Preface

Quid Pro Quo. Something exchanged for something else. To solve these puzzles, you exchange English clues for Latin words that you select from a list. The list includes a few "red herrings" to make the choices more challenging. You may find that reading the list before starting the puzzle will help you solve the puzzle faster. For a greater challenge, you may want to cover the list and try going ahead on your own.

Eight of the fifty puzzles involve well-known phrases such as *in medias res*, where the English meaning of the phrase is given and you are to decide which of the listed words completes the phrase. Four of the fifty are "reverse" puzzles, where you put an English word into the grid. Solutions to all the puzzles start on page 51.

You will notice that the puzzles have been numbered in Latin style (i.e., with Roman numerals). An explanation of the Roman numeral system appears among the Addenda, which not surprisingly is Latin for "things added." Other bonus features in the Addenda section include commonly used abbreviations for Latin words and phrases, and several state mottoes in Latin.

If you took Latin long ago, you will enjoy discovering how much of it you remember. If you have never studied Latin at all, the puzzles will expand your English vocabulary. Besides, you will learn a lot of Latin without even trying.

During a year's trial of these puzzles, the most surprising responses came when copies found their way into the hands of people long out of school. The puzzles have entertained travelers on long plane trips and relieved boredom for shut-ins. As one retired businesswoman said, "It's fun to find unsuspected assets in the brain!"

B.W.R.
V.F.A.

Acknowledgments

The Latin vocabulary used in most of these puzzles, used with permission of the publishers, is from the following two well-known first-year Latin textbooks: *Latin for Americans, First Book,* seventh edition, by B. L. Ullman, Charles Henderson Jr., and Norman E. Henry, published by Glencoe of Macmillan/McGraw Hill, 1990; and *Latin via Ovid, A First Course,* second edition, by Norma Goldman and Jacob Nyenhuis, published by Wayne State University Press, 1982.

We would like to thank the following people for the support they have given to this project: Linda Armour, Patricia Axt, John Ervin Jr., Gary Gabriel, and David P. Harris. We especially appreciate the outstanding help of our editor, Christopher Brown.

I. PRIMA CHARTA – *FIRST MAP*

ACROSS

5. I look at, watch
6. map
8. peninsula
10. island
11. friend
12. I desire
14. king
15. poet
17. I flee
19. first
20. I love
21. I carry
22. I live

DOWN

1. land, country
2. new
3. large
4. fearful, shy
7. I change
8. beautiful, pretty
9. where
12. god
13. good
16. daughter
17. story
18. I tell

Select from these words:

AMICA	FUGITO	POETA	TERRA
AMO	HABITO	PORTO	TIMIDA
BONUS	INSULA	PRIMUS	TRANSFORMO
CHARTA	LUDO	PUELLA	UBI
DESIDERO	MAGNUS	PULCHRA	
DEUS	NARRO	REX	
FABULA	NOVA	SPECTO	
FILIA	PAENINSULA	TAURUS	

II. AGRICOLA BONUS – *A GOOD FARMER*

			1		2							
			3			4		5			6	
	7					8						
9												
					10							
		11			12							
13												
	14	15		16								
17							18		19			
20					21							22
									23			
					24							
25			26									
					27							

ACROSS
3. where
8. I look at
9. long
12. large
13. many
14. farmer
19. not
20. horse
21. I work
23. life
25. I love
26. water
27. forest

DOWN
1. hard
2. road, way
4. it is
5. slave
6. I carry
7. fortune
10. family
11. and
15. I praise
16. island
17. land, earth
18. good
19. new
22. report
24. bad

Select from these words:

AGRICOLA	EST	LONGUS	REGALIS
AMO	ET	MAGNUS	SERVUS
AQUA	FAMA	MALUS	SILVA
BONUS	FAMILIA	MULTUS	SPECTO
CARRUS	FORTUNA	NON	TERRA
DURUS	GAUDEO	NOVUS	UBI
EQUUS	INSULA	PARVUS	VIA
ERAT	LABORO	PORTO	VITA

III. FEMINA IRATA – *AN ANGRY WOMAN*

ACROSS

1. I owe
3. I work
5. angry
8. picture
9. I write
12. teacher
14. I teach
16. wisdom
17. rash
20. I reply
22. forest
24. students
25. wool
26. I deny
27. I shout

DOWN

1. lord, master
2. I praise
4. I affirm
6. farmer
7. I call
10. I try
11. I shape
13. experience
15. woodland spirit
18. woman
19. I copy, imitate
21. name
23. life

Select from these words:

AFFIRMO	DOCEO	MAGISTER	SCRIBO
AGRICOLA	EXPERIENTIA	MONSTRO	SIMULO
BENE	FEMINA	NEGO	SILVA
CASA	FORMO	NOMEN	TELA
CLAMO	IRATA	NYMPHA	TEMERARIA
DEBEO	LANA	PICTURA	TEMPTO
DISCIPULI	LABORO	RESPONDEO	VITA
DOMINUS	LAUDO	SAPIENTIA	VOCO

3

IV. QUINTA HORA – *FIFTH HOUR*

ACROSS

3. number
7. wrong, injury
8. I seize, occupy
10. victory
11. I give, donate
12. I point out, demonstrate
13. letter
16. I entrust
19. battle
20. money
23. clear
25. I test
26. form
27. queen

DOWN

1. I urge on, incite
2. care
3. I sail, navigate
4. memory
5. fifth
6. province
9. level
14. friend
15. hour
17. I report
18. I fight
21. ship
22. pleasing
23. supply
24. wave

Select from these words:

AMICUS	FORMA	MEMORIA	PECUNIA	REGINA
CIBUS	GRATUS	MONSTRO	PLANUS	SERVO
CLARUS	HORA	NAUTA	PROBO	UNDA
COPIA	INCITO	NAVIGO	PROVINCIA	VICTORIA
CURA	INIURIA	NUMERUS	PUGNA	
DONO	LITTERA	NUNTIO	PUGNO	
FILIA	MANDO	OCCUPO	QUINTUS	

V. OCULUS CLARUS – *A CLEAR EYE*

ACROSS

3. son
5. I hang
7. flame
8. I stop
9. I beg, pray
10. gift
11. many
12. I stand
13. happy, blessed
15. very small
19. eye
20. I decorate
21. reason, cause

DOWN

1. long
2. temple
3. family
4. clear
5. boy
6. power
7. fortune
14. one
15. smaller
16. bad
17. reputation
18. I change

Select from these words:

BEATUS	FORTUNA	OCULUS	STO
CAUSA	LONGA	OPTIMA	TEMPLUM
CLARUS	MALA	ORO	UNUS
DONUM	MINIMA	ORNO	VIA
FAMA	MINOR	PENDEO	
FAMILIA	MONEO	POTENTIA	
FILIUS	MULTUS	PROHIBEO	
FLAMMA	MUTO	PUER	

VI. TEMPUS FUGIT – *TIME FLIES*

ACROSS

3. with highest honors (*summa cum* ____)
5. stiffness after death (*rigor* ____)
7. entirely (*in* ____)
9. from the library of (*ex* ____)
12. one of a kind (*sui* ____)
15. voice of the people (*vox* ____)
16. solid ground (*terra* ____)
18. in the midst of things (*in medias* ____)
19. a necessity (*sine qua* ____)

DOWN

1. unchanged position (*status* ____)
2. in the womb (*in* ____)
4. Buyer beware! (*caveat* ____)
5. not of sound mind (*non compos* ____)
6. intrinsically, of itself (*per* ____)
8. way of life (*modus* ____)
10. my fault (*mea* ____)
11. before the war (*ante* ____)
13. modern man (*homo* ____)
14. Beware of the dog! (*cave* ____)
17. confidentially (*sub* ____)

Select from these words:

ALIA	GENERIS	NON	TOTO
BELLI	IGITUR	POPULI	UTERO
BELLUM	LAUDE	QUO	VINO
BOREALIS	LIBRIS	RES	VIVENDI
CANEM	MEMORIAM	ROSA	
CULPA	MENTIS	SAPIENS	
EMPTOR	MORTIS	SE	
FIRMA	MUTANDIS	TENEBRIS	

VII. LINGUA BARBARA – *A FOREIGN LANGUAGE*

ACROSS

4. fatherland
5. I depart
6. I am
9. I liberate, free
11. son
13. I have
15. teacher
17. I hold
18. prisoner
19. high, steep
20. settler
23. house
25. I remain
28. foreign
29. I deserve, merit
30. I teach
31. tongue, language
32. I scare, terrify

DOWN

1. matter
2. sign
3. I call
7. I move
8. man
10. glory
12. training, discipline
14. year
16. comrade
19. mind
21. always
22. I see
24. I increase
26. I live
27. boy

Select from these words:

ALTUS	COLONUS	LINGUA	PATRIA	TERREO
ANIMUS	DISCIPLINA	MAGISTER	PUER	VIDEO
ANNUS	DOCEO	MANEO	SACER	VIR
AUGEO	FILIUS	MATERIA	SEMPER	VOCO
BARBARUS	GLORIA	MEREO	SIGNUM	
CAPTIVUS	HABEO	MIGRO	SOCIUS	
CASA	HABITO	MOVEO	SUM	
CASTRA	LIBERO	NOSTER	TENEO	

VIII. CAMPUS PLANUS – *A LEVEL FIELD*

ACROSS
1. mother
5. disaster
7. field
10. I freeze, stiffen
13. last
16. funerals
17. quickly
20. I cry, weep
21. wicked, evil

DOWN
2. horse
3. enough
4. I honor
6. school, class
8. statue
9. people
10. I call together, summon
11. complaint
12. I train, exercise
14. level, flat
15. I leave behind
18. word
19. I fly

Select from these words:

CAMPUS	HONORO	POPULUS	STATUA
CELERITER	IUVO	PROFANUS	ULTIMUS
CONGELO	LACRIMO	QUERELLA	VERBUM
CONVOCO	MAGIS	RELINQUO	VOLO
DIGNUS	MATER	ROGO	
EQUUS	MORA	RUINA	
EXERCEO	PLANUS	SATIS	
FUNERA	POENA	SCHOLA	

IX. CONCORDIA VERA – *TRUE HARMONY*

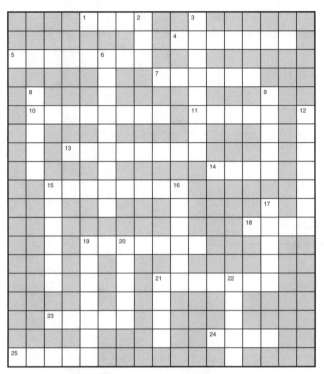

ACROSS
1. weapons, arms
4. messenger
5. I look out for, await
7. war
10. duty
11. cause
13. end
14. I retreat
15. aid
18. I rule
19. master
21. people
23. I come
24. I lead
25. I owe

DOWN
2. I do
3. public
6. harmony
8. place
9. I do, make
12. I bring about
15. even, calm
16. I hasten
17. true
19. I defend
20. I send
21. I put, place
22. wide

Select from these words:

ACCIPIO	CEDO	EXSPECTO	NUNTIUS	REGO
AEQUUS	CONCORDIA	FACIO	OFFICIUM	TERMINUS
AGO	DEBEO	INVENIO	PONO	VENIO
ARMA	DEFENDO	LATUS	POPULUS	VERUS
AUXILIUM	DOMINUS	LOCUS	PRETIUM	
BELLUM	DUCO	MATURO	PUBLICUS	
CAUSA	EFFICIO	MITTO	PULCHER	

X. EQUUS FERUS – *A WILD HORSE (Review Puzzle)*

ACROSS

1. field
4. I breathe
7. horse
8. complaint
10. I wander
13. kind
14. teacher
17. I call
18. farmer
21. gift
22. I live
23. wisdom
28. help
29. name
31. eye
33. son
34. I stand
35. I decorate
36. I retain
39. I hang
41. I shout
42. word
43. land

DOWN

2. star
3. happy
5. power
6. prone
9. wave
10. I await
11. daughter
12. forest
13. arm
15. I write
16. wild
19. evil
20. neighboring
24. friend
25. I tell
26. I train
27. I see
30. I shape
32. sleep
37. I hold
38. mother
40. I pray

Select from these words:

AGRICOLA	DESIDERO	FILIUS	ORNO	RETINEO	SUSPIRO
AMICUS	DONUM	FORMO	ORO	SAPIENTIA	TENEO
AUXILIUM	EQUUS	HABITO	PENDEO	SCRIBO	TERRA
BEATUS	ERRO	MAGISTER	POTENTIA	SILVA	UNDA
BENIGNUS	EXERCEO	MATER	PROFANUS	SIMULO	VERBUM
BRACCHIUM	EXSPECTO	NARRO	PRONUS	SOMNUS	VICINUS
CAMPUS	FERUS	NOMEN	PULCHER	STELLA	VIDEO
CLAMO	FILIA	OCULUS	QUERELLA	STO	VOCO

XI. VIR BENIGNUS – *A KIND MAN*

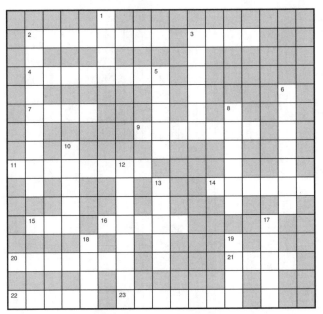

ACROSS

2. kind, benign
3. flight
4. forever, eternal
7. I hide
9. I devote
11. help
14. no, none
15. man
16. across
20. paper
21. wave
22. I hold, retain
23. I breathe

DOWN

1. field
2. arm, limb
3. I flee, avoid
5. I stay
6. woodland goat-man
8. thick, dense
10. unhappy, miserable
12. shady
13. sound
17. I see
18. I wander
19. I think

Select from these words:

AETERNUM	DENSUS	PAPYRUS	UMBROSUS
AGER	DEVOVEO	PUTO	UNDA
AUXILIUM	ERRO	RIPA	VIR
BENIGNUS	FUGA	SATYRUS	VIDEO
BRACCHIUM	FUGITO	SONUS	
CELO	MANEO	SUSPIRO	
CERA	MISER	TENEO	
CONCILIUM	NULLUS	TRANS	

XII. SENTENTIA FIRMA – *A FIRM OPINION*

ACROSS
1. few
5. constant
8. opinion
9. strong, firm
10. I read
11. I hold together
14. remaining
15. late
16. suitable, convenient
20. I begin
21. with
22. book
23. I flee
24. poet
25. I draw, drag

DOWN
2. I call
3. I hear
4. god
6. guard, protection
7. I lead back
12. word
13. changing, varying
16. I call together
17. middle
18. leisure
19. I write

Select from these words:

APPELLO	DEUS	OTIUM	SCRIBO
AUDIO	FINITIMUS	PAUCI	SENTENTIA
COMMITTO	FIRMUS	PERPETUUS	STUDIUM
COMMODUS	FUGIO	POETA	TARDUS
CONTINEO	INCIPIO	PRAESIDIUM	TRAHO
CONVENIO	LEGO	PROPERO	VALEO
CONVOCO	LIBER	REDUCO	VARIUS
CUM	MEDIUS	RELIQUUS	VERBUM

XIII. TERRA FIRMA – *SOLID GROUND*

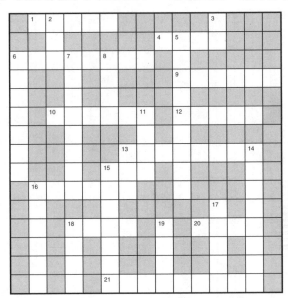

ACROSS

1. in the work cited (____ *citato*)
4. without a day being set, indefinitely adjourned (____ *die*)
6. cast of a play (*dramatis* ____)
9. by heads, for each individual (*per* ____)
10. northern dawn, northern lights (____ *borealis*)
12. an objectionable person (*persona non* ____)
13. peace be with you (*pax* ____)
16. after death (*post* ____)
18. a rare bird, prodigy (*rara* ____)
20. something in return, compensation (____ *pro quo*)
21. to infinity, indefinitely (*ad* ____)

DOWN

2. by the year, annually (____ *annum*)
3. in fact, actually (____ *facto*)
5. region or subject about which nothing is known (*terra* ____)
6. always ready (*semper* ____)
7. it does not follow, illogical reference (*non* ____)
8. anew, afresh (*de* ____)
11. love conquers all (*omnia vincit* ____)
14. after midday (*post* ____)
15. the body of the crime (*corpus* ____)
16. author's chief work (____ *opus*)
17. time flies (*tempus* ____)
18. fostering mother, university attended (____ *mater*)
19. I came, I saw, I conquered (*veni*, ____, *vici*)

Select from these words:

ALMA	FUGIT	NOVO	SINE
AMOR	GRATA	OPERE	TABULA
AURORA	IN	PARATUS	VIDI
AVIS	INCOGNITA	PER	VOBISCUM
CAPITA	INFINITUM	PERSONAE	
DE	MAGNUM	QUID	
DELICTI	MERIDIEM	RES	
EX	MORTEM	SEQUITUR	

XIV. DELECTAMENTUM! – *A DELIGHT!*

ACROSS

3. winner
7. word
8. feeling
9. star
12. human
13. I invoke
15. figure
20. pleasing (to)
22. wild, feral
25. neighboring
26. I care for
27. delight
29. I transport
30. sleep

DOWN

1. well known, noted, familiar
2. born
4. cause
5. time
6. alone
10. I stretch out
11. bent over, prone
14. garment, clothes
16. injury, hurt, wrong
17. I approach
18. neglected
19. grassy
21. I hold back, retain
23. I await
24. animal
25. voice
28. wrath

Select from these words:

ALIUS	FERUS	NATUS	SOMNUS	VICINUS
ANIMAL	FIGURA	NEGLECTUS	STELLA	VICTOR
APPROPINQUO	GRATUS	NOTUS	TEMPUS	VOX
CAELUM	HERBOSUS	POENA	TENDO	
CAUSA	HUMANUS	PRONUS	TRANSPORTO	
CURO	INIURIA	RETINEO	URSA	
DELECTAMENTUM	INVOCO	SENSA	VERBUM	
EXSPECTO	IRA	SOLUS	VESTIMENTUM	

XV. MODUS INIMICUS – *AN UNFRIENDLY MANNER*

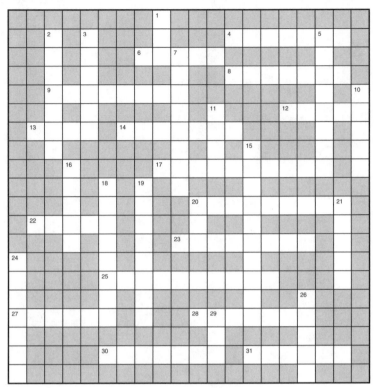

ACROSS

4. I hold, obtain
6. I am away, absent
8. untouched, fresh
9. unfriendly
12. I desire
13. I ask
14. I take back, receive
17. kindness
20. danger
22. among, between
23. I save, preserve
25. I stop, interrupt
27. first
28. I remain
30. I proceed
31. nature

DOWN

1. under
2. I hold back
3. I hesitate, doubt
5. example
7. I hold up, maintain
10. I warn, remind
11. without
15. diligence
16. gate
18. excellent (note: English derivative has opposite meaning)
19. I allow
20. before, in front of, for
21. unhappy, poor
24. I put forward, propose
26. manner
29. I

Select from these words:

ABSUM	EGREGIUS	MODUS	PORTA	RETINEO
BENEFICIUM	EXEMPLUM	MONEO	PRIMUS	SINE
CONSERVO	INIMICUS	NATURA	PRO	SUB
CUPIO	INTEGER	OBTINEO	PROCEDO	SUSTINEO
DILIGENTIA	INTER	PERICULUM	PRODUCO	
DUBITO	INTERMITTO	PERMITTO	PROPONO	
EDUCO	LIBER	PERMOVEO	RECIPIO	
EGO	MISER	PETO	REMANEO	

XVI. SENEX IMPIUS – *A WICKED OLD MAN*

ACROSS

2. old man, woman
5. pool
7. part
9. I
10. I doubt, hesitate
11. priest, priestess
13. bowl
15. it leafs out
19. miracle
21. guardian, keeper
23. man
24. done, made
25. upright, just
26. reward, premium
29. father
30. wine
31. rest

DOWN

1. I enter
2. I sit
3. tree
4. year
6. greater
8. goose
12. husband, wife, spouse
14. king
16. true
17. I catch, seize
18. fish
20. place
22. leg
24. end
25. wicked, impious
27. between, among
28. I live

Select from these words:

ANNUS	EGO	INTER	PATER	SEDEO
ANSER	FACTUS	INTRO	PISCIS	SENEX
ARBOR	FINIS	IUSTUS	PRAEMIUM	STAGNUM
CONIUNX	FRONDET	LOCUS	PREHENDEO	VASTO
CRATER	HOMO	MAIOREM	RECEPTUS	VERUS
CUSTOS	IMPERO	MEMBRUM	REQUIES	VINUM
DUBITO	IMMENSUS	MIRACULUM	REX	VIVO
DUO	IMPIUS	PARS	SACERDOS	

XVII. MILES PARATUS – *A READY SOLDIER*

ACROSS

1. prepared
4. foot
5. law
6. peace
10. I carry across
11. soldier
14. flight
15. I bind
18. I hinder
20. deed
21. farthest
22. sure, fixed
24. man
25. health
26. I stand

DOWN

2. I leave behind, abandon
3. king
4. I press
7. I go before
8. I foresee
9. I consult
12. space
13. third
16. known, familiar
17. I lead across
19. fearful, shy
22. I shout
23. I ask

Select from these words:

ANTECEDO	FUGA	PAX	SPATIUM
CERNO	HOMO	PES	STO
CERTUS	IMPEDIO	PREMO	TERTIUS
CLAMO	LEX	PROVIDEO	TIMIDUS
CONSULO	LIGO	RELINQUO	TRADUCO
EXPEDIO	MILES	REX	TRANSPORTO
FACTUM	NOTUS	ROGO	ULTIMUS
DUX	PARATUS	SALUS	VERTO

XVIII. RARA AVIS – *A RARE BIRD*

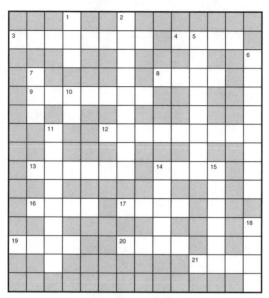

AROSS

3. in memory (*in ____*)
4. in the place of a parent (*in ____ parentis*)
8. enjoy the present (*carpe ____*)
9. a title (feminine) given especially to a retired professor (*____*)
12. out of the depths (*de ____*)
13. much in little (*____ in parvo*)
14. and others (*et ____*)
16. in wine there is truth (*in ____ veritas*)
17. before noon (*____ meridiem*)
19. not more beyond, acme, culmination (*ne ____ ultra*)
20. day of wrath, day of judgment (*dies ____*)
21. I do not wish to contest, plea in criminal cases (*____ contendere*)

DOWN

1. for this (particular purpose) (*ad ____*)
2. holy of holies (*sanctum ____*)
5. manner of working (*modus ____*)
6. Master of Arts (degree) (*____ Artium*)
7. (so much) by the day (*____ diem*)
10. a god out of a machine, providential intervention (*deus ____ machina*)
11. one out of many (USA motto) (*e ____ unum*)
14. through hardships to the stars (*per aspera ad ____*)
15. from the beginning (*ab ____*)
18. which was to be demonstrated (*____ erat demonstrandum*)

Select from these words:

ALII	IRAE	PER	VINO
ANTE	LOCO	PLURIBUS	VIVA
ASTRA	MAGISTER	PLUS	
DIEM	MEMORIAM	PROFUNDIS	
EMERITA	MULTUM	QUOD	
EX	NOLO	RASA	
HOC	OPERANDI	SANCTORUM	
INITIO	PARES	SUM	

XIX. NOX OBSCURA – *A DARK NIGHT*

ACROSS

4. image
6. white
8. body
9. kiss
13. cave
14. other
17. I carry back, report
18. medicine
21. color
22. mountain
24. dark, obscure
25. river
27. head
32. laurel tree
33. finger
35. sister
36. I grow, increase
38. maiden
39. I touch
40. hand
41. wound

DOWN

1. I make, do
2. bank of a river
3. I stop, desist
5. art, skill
6. water
7. love
10. satisfied, content
11. I seek, ask
12. I consume, devour
14. another
15. bow
16. grief
19. sharp
20. enemy
23. young person, youth
24. dull, blunt
26. night
28. I say
29. flower
30. liveliness, force, vigor
31. music
34. leaf
37. branch
42. sun

Select from these words:

ACUTUS	COLOR	DUX	IUVENIS	OSCULUM	TANGO
ALBUS	CONTENTUS	FACIO	LAURUS	PETO	TELUM
ALIUS	CORPUS	FIGO	MANUS	PUDOR	VIGOR
ALTER	CRESCO	FLOR	MEDICINA	RAMUS	VIRGO
AMOR	DESISTO	FLUMEN	MONS	REPORTO	VULNUS
AQUA	DEVORO	FOLIUM	MUSICA	RIPA	
ARCUS	DICO	HOSTIS	NOX	SOL	
ARS	DIGITUS	HUMO	OBSCURUS	SOROR	
CAPUT	DOLOR	IMAGO	OBTUSUS	SPELUNCA	

XX. ITER FACILE – *AN EASY ROAD*

ACROSS
1. head
3. father
4. wound
5. body
8. swift
11. enemy
12. river
13. I close
14. I stretch
16. justice, right
17. authority
20. all, every
23. ship
24. author
25. manliness, courage
26. I excel

DOWN
1. citizen
2. order, rank
3. after
6. I answer
7. time
9. name
10. freedom
12. brave, strong
13. I establish, make firm
15. easy
18. citizenship, state
19. mountain
21. sea
22. journey, road

Select from these words:

AUCTOR	CONFICIO	HOSTIS	NOMEN	RESPONDEO
AUCTORITAS	CONFIRMO	ITER	OMNIS	SUPERO
CAPUT	CORPUS	IUS	ORDO	TEMPUS
CELER	FACILIS	LIBERTAS	PAR	TENDO
CIVIS	FAMILIARIS	MARE	PATER	VIRTUS
CIVITAS	FLUMEN	MONS	PELLO	VULNUS
CLAUDO	FORTIS	NAVIS	POST	

XXI. DOMUS ALBA – *A WHITE HOUSE*

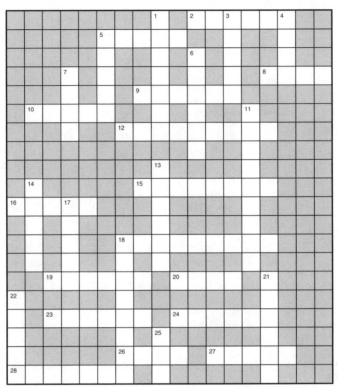

ACROSS

2. I seek, ask
5. I deceive
8. death
9. worthy
10. I come
12. track, footstep
15. I leave behind, relinquish
16. I draw, drag
18. advice, plan
19. parent
20. I drink
23. wall
24. crack
26. road, path, way
27. house
28. I speak softly

DOWN

1. sword
3. white
4. I wish for, desire
5. I flee
6. I feel, sense
7. fountain
11. purple
13. recently
14. before, earlier
17. grass
18. I meet
21. time
22. fruit, apple
25. lion

Select from these words:

ALBUS	FISSUM	MURMURO	QUAESO	VENIO
BIBO	FONS	OPTO	RADIX	VESTIGIUM
CONSILIUM	FUGIO	PARENS	RECENS	VICINUS
CONVENIO	GLADIUS	PARIES	RELINQUO	
CRUENTUS	HERBA	POMUM	SENTIO	
DIGNUS	ITER	PRIOR	TEMPUS	
DOMUS	LEO	PURPUREUS	TRAHO	
FALLO	MORS	QUAERO	VELAMEN	

XXII. DIES DURA – *A ROUGH DAY*

ACROSS

1. fruit of a tree
6. I free
7. I conquer
9. fire
11. I hear
13. day
14. third
15. hour
17. thing
18. name
20. house
24. left (hand), adverse
26. end
27. sister
28. hard, rough
29. I lead
31. dull
32. I carry off
36. body
37. I drag
38. guilt, fault
39. I seek
40. every, all

DOWN

2. hand
3. I drink
4. tree
5. worthy
8. I believe
10. I sit
12. young person
14. I finish, end
16. year
19. I move
21. dead
22. I sing
23. I increase
25. cave
27. I know, understand
30. I hope for, wish
33. I do, make
34. ear
35. road, way

Select from these words:

AMOR	CREDO	FACIO	LIBERO	POMUM	SPELUNCA
ANNUS	CRESCO	FINIS	MANUS	QUAERO	TERMINO
ARBOR	CULPA	FLUMEN	MORTUUS	RAPIO	TERTIUS
AUDIO	DIES	HOMO	MOVEO	RES	TRAHO
AURIS	DIGNUS	HORA	NOMEN	SCIO	VENIO
BIBO	DOMUS	IGNIS	OBTUSUS	SEDEO	VERUS
CANTO	DUCO	ITER	OMNIS	SINISTER	VINCO
CORPUS	DURUS	IUVENIS	OPTO	SOROR	VINUM

XXIII. COR NOBILIS – *A NOBLE HEART*

ACROSS
1. I breathe
4. I touch
5. brother
8. one
9. I fear
10. I sit
13. noble
16. heart
18. mother
19. nothing
21. I intercept
23. other, another
24. winter
25. power

DOWN
1. sister
2. part
3. whole
6. I send back
7. I run
10. alone
11. common
12. I drive out
13. neither
14. kneeling down, punishment
15. uncertain
17. birth, kind
20. I break
22. death

Select from these words:

ALIUS	FRATER	NEUTER	SOROR
COLO	GENUS	NIHIL	SPERO
COMMUNIS	HIEMS	NOBILIS	SPIRO
COR	IDEM	PARS	SUPPLICIUM
CURRO	INCERTUS	POTESTAS	TANGO
EXPELLO	INTERCIPIO	REMITTO	TIMEO
EXPUGNO	MATER	SEDEO	TOTUS
FRANGO	MORS	SOLUS	UNUS

XXIV. AD HOC – *FOR THIS PURPOSE*

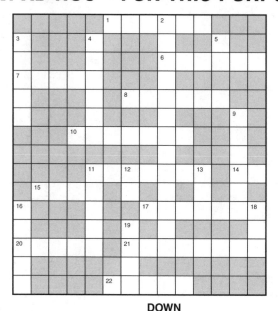

ACROSS

1. sound of mind (____ *mentis*)
6. clean slate, an erased tablet (____ *rasa*)
7. he himself said it (*ipse* ____)
8. to err is human (____ *humanum est*)
10. to the point of nausea (*ad* ____)
11. art of poetry (*ars* ____)
14. that is (____ *est*)
15. by the living voice, orally (____ *voce*)
17. always faithful (*semper* ____)
20. Larger Dog (constellation) (____ *major*)
21. reduction to absurdity (*reductio ad* ____)
22. with great praise or distinction (*magna cum* ____)

DOWN

2. father of a family (____)
3. Whither goest thou? (*quo* ____)
4. farthest Thule, unknown land or region (____ *Thule*)
5. and thou, too, Brutus (*et* ____, *Brute*)
9. in the year of our Lord (*anno* ____)
11. first among his equals (*primus inter* ____)
12. from one party or side (____ *parte*)
13. Hail and farewell! (____ *atque vale*)
16. at first view, based on first impression (*prima* ____)
18. I think, therefore I am (*cogito ergo* ____)
19. proportionally (*pro* ____)

Select from these words:

ABSURDUM	EX	PATERFAMILIAS	VADIS
AVE	FACIE	POETICA	VIVA
CANIS	FIDELIS	POST	
COMPOS	ID	RATA	
DE	LAUDE	SUM	
DIXIT	MUTANDIS	TABULA	
DOMINI	NAUSEAM	TU	
ERRARE	PARES	ULTIMA	

XXV. VICTORIA INCERTA – *AN UNCERTAIN VICTORY*

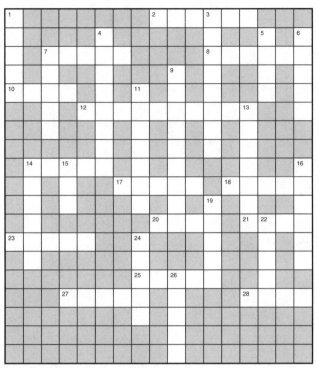

ACROSS

2. I call, name
7. I capture, take
8. I close
10. I sound
12. memorial, reminder
14. guilt, fault
17. I send
18. I hear
20. urn, vase
21. I know
23. hard, harsh
25. I move, stir
27. I seize, carry off
28. hour

DOWN

1. fire
3. unsure
4. victory
5. care, concern
6. horn, end, tip
7. ashes
9. watcher
11. boldness, audacity
13. dead
14. running, course
15. law
16. I crown
19. I condemn
22. I blame
24. rumor, hearsay
26. I conquer, defeat

Select from these words:

ADDUCO	COMES	DURUS	MOVEO	SPECTATOR
AUDACIA	CORNU	HORA	NOMINO	URNA
AUDIO	CORONO	IGNIS	PERICULUM	VICTORIA
AVUS	CULPA	INCERTUS	PONO	VINCO
CAPIO	CULPO	LEX	RAPIO	
CERTAMEN	CURA	MITTO	RUMOR	
CINIS	CURSUS	MONUMENTUM	SCIO	
CLAUDO	DAMNO	MORTUUS	SONO	

XXVI. LABOR GRAVIS – *HEAVY WORK*

ACROSS

2. light
7. I think
8. I threaten, take a firm stand
9. work, hardship
10. I throw
14. second
15. I show
17. I hold fast, cling
19. month
20. voice
21. just
24. I stand still, stop
25. force, violence
26. another's, strange

DOWN

1. I say
3. I feel
4. city
5. I overcome, surprise
6. heavy, severe
11. I struggle
12. I come through, arrive
13. duty, service
16. I keep from, prevent
18. sharp, keen
22. I know
23. I loosen, take apart

Select from these words:

ACER	IACIO	OPPRIMO	SECUNDUS
ALIENUS	INSTO	OSTENDO	SENTIO
CONSISTO	IUSTUS	PERVENIO	SOLVO
CONTENDO	LABOR	PROHIBEO	TARDUS
DICO	LIBER	PRETIUM	URBS
EXCEDO	LEVIS	PUTO	VERUS
GRAVIS	MENSIS	REDUCO	VIS
HAEREO	MUNUS	SCIO	VOX

XXVII. SECUNDUS AUCTOR – *A SECOND AUTHOR*

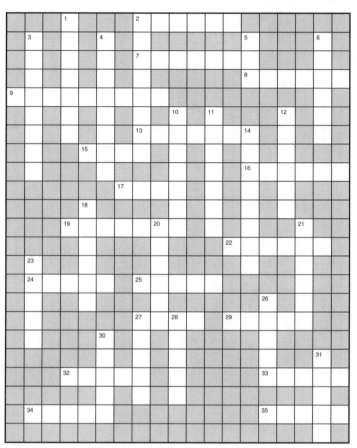

ACROSS
2. page
7. to the side, obliquely
8. sign
9. thought, opinion
13. third
15. I lead
16. crime, sin
17. day
19. secretly
22. author
24. high, deep
25. gold
27. I wash, lave
29. hero
32. by chance
33. each, every, all
34. I sin
35. rock, stone

DOWN
1. unwilling
2. I promise
3. unfavorable, adverse
4. ruinous
5. thing
6. I rejoice, enjoy
10. I go across, pass over
11. green
12. easily
14. following, second
18. middle of
20. board, plank, table
21. door post
23. I throw
26. I believe, trust
27. book
28. pardon, favor
30. I run
31. at the same time

Select from these words:

ADVERSUS	CURRO	GAUDEO	OBLIQUE	SAXUM	TENDO
ALTUS	DAMNOSUS	HEROS	OMNIS	SECRETO	TERTIUS
AUCTOR	DIES	IACIO	PAGINA	SECUNDUS	TRANSEO
AURUM	DUCO	INVITUS	PECCO	SENTENTIA	VENIA
CARPO	FACILE	LAVO	POSTIS	SIGNUS	VIRIDIS
CREDO	FLUO	LIBER	PROMITTO	SIMUL	
CRIMEN	FORTE	MEDIUS	RES	TABULA	

XXVIII. ORATIO DIFFICILIS – *A DIFFICULT SPEECH*

ACROSS

2. highest
5. farther
8. condition, terms
10. farthest, last
11. lower
12. I grant
14. power
15. suitable, fit
16. unlike
20. people, nation
23. I catch sight of
26. speech
27. I join
28. humble

DOWN

1. I believe
3. thousand
4. I determine, establish
6. nearest, next
7. hundred
9. difficult
13. work, labor, product of work
17. like, similar
18. I judge
19. one's own
21. I explain
22. envoy
24. I arrange, provide
25. region

Select from these words:

APTUS	EXTREMUS	LEGATUS	REPELLO
CENTUM	GENS	MILLE	SIMILIS
CONDITIO	HUMILIS	NEMO	STATUO
CONSPICIO	IMPERIUM	OPUS	SUMMUS
CREDO	INFERIOR	ORATIO	TRIBUO
DIFFICILIS	INSTRUO	PROPRIUS	ULTERIOR
DISSIMILIS	IUDICO	PROXIMUS	UTILIS
EXPLICO	IUNGO	REGIO	VINCO

XXIX. ARS POETICA – *THE ART OF POETRY*

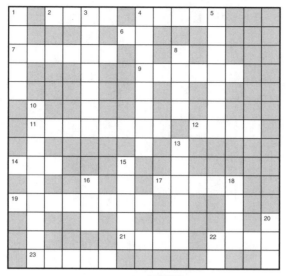

ACROSS

2. rest in peace (*requiescat in* ____)
4. nature abhors a vacuum (*natura abhorret a* ____)
6. by law, rightfully (____ *jure*)
7. in the nature of things (*in rerum* ____)
9. art (is) long, life short (*ars longa, vita* ____)
11. not here, absent (*in* ____)
12. for the public good (*pro* ____ *publico*)
14. with praise or distinction (____ *laude*)
17. in glass (a reaction carried out in a laboratory culture dish) (*in* ____)
19. from the chair, authoritatively (*ex* ____)
21. love for one's country (____ *patriae*)
22. to be rather than to seem (____ *quam videri*)
23. while I breathe, I hope (*dum* ____, *spero*)

DOWN

1. work conquers all things (*labor* ____ *vincit*)
3. a sound mind in a sound body (*mens sana in* ____ *sano*)
4. word for word (____)
5. by virtue of one's office (*ex* ____)
8. note well, take notice (*nota* ____)
10. we who are about to die salute thee (*morituri te* ____)
13. let us then be joyful (*gaudeamus* ____)
15. for the sake of form (*pro* ____)
16. God willing (____ *volente*)
18. burden of proof (____ *probandi*)
20. by the hundred percent (____ *centum*)
22. and the following (____ *sequens*)

Select from these words:

ABSENTIA	CORPORE	FORMA	PACE
AMOR	CUM	IGITUR	PER
AVE	DE	LAPSUS	SALUTAMUS
BENE	DEO	NATURA	SPIRO
BONO	DIES	OFFICIO	VACUO
BREVIS	ESSE	OMNIA	VERBATIM
CATHEDRA	ET	ONUS	VITRO

XXX. AURIS HUMANA – *THE HUMAN EAR*

ACROSS

3. I cut off
5. I sing, make music
6. wind
8. I end, finish
10. I say, speak
11. I bear, carry, do
12. lyre
14. I wonder at, admire
15. judgment
17. ear
20. I blow into
21. unjust, unfair
22. judge
23. I disdain
24. I till, cultivate
25. I am silent
26. foreign, rude
27. I allow, suffer

DOWN

1. right, skillful
2. I free
4. I decorate, adorn
7. human, humane
9. I dig, excavate
11. gem, jewel
13. I turn
16. I whisper into
18. I put back
19. left (hand), adverse

Select from these words:

AURIS	DEXTER	IUDEX	REPONO
BARBARUS	EFFODIO	IUDICIUM	RESECO
CANTO	GEMMA	LIBERO	SINISTER
CARMEN	GERO	LOQUOR	TACEO
COLO	HUMANUS	LYRA	TERMINO
CONOR	IMMURMURO	MIROR	VENTUS
CONTEMNO	INFLO	ORIOR	VEREOR
DECORO	INIUSTUS	PATIOR	VERTO

XXXI. PRIMA LUX – *FIRST LIGHT*

ACROSS

5. senate
6. over, above
7. I hate, despise
9. I explore, investigate
11. I desert, forsake
13. I show
15. army
17. business
20. leader
21. I injure, hurt
22. appearance, aspect
24. front, forehead
25. I command
26. home

DOWN

1. I send ahead
2. reason
3. light
4. I climb
8. I understand
10. thing, matter
12. I give back
14. day
15. I train, exercise
16. I survive, remain
18. attack, impulse
19. hand
23. hope

Select from these words:

ASCENDO	EXERCITUS	MANUS	RATIO
CASUS	EXPLORO	NEGOTIUM	REDDO
DEMONSTRO	FRONS	NOCEO	RES
DESERO	IMPERO	POSTQUAM	SENATUS
DESPICIO	IMPETUS	PRAEFICIO	SPECIES
DIES	INTELLEGO	PRAEMITTO	SPES
DOMUS	INTERCLUDO	PRAESUM	SUPER
EXERCEO	LUX	PRINCEPS	SUPERSUM

XXXII. SEMPER FELIX – *ALWAYS HAPPY*

ACROSS

4. I do, drive
5. I reweave, unravel
8. hard, harsh, bitter
10. I regain, take back
13. I am amazed
15. huge
16. step
18. circle, wheel
20. monster
22. spirit, soul
23. breeze, air
26. cruel, bloody
28. mute, silent
29. kingdom, rule
30. I receive, accept
31. outcome, end
32. I look back, look behind
33. twin, double

DOWN

1. I weep, mourn for
2. happy, fortunate
3. I go out, depart
4. I dare
6. torch
7. hard, difficult, arduous
9. I die, perish
11. I find, discover
12. I turn back
13. highest, upper
14. unhappy
17. shade, shadow, spirit
19. fate
20. marriage
21. wedding
24. eager
25. omen, portent
27. snake

Select from these words:

ACCIPIO	CRUDELIS	HERBA	NUPTIAE	RESPICIO
ACER	DENS	INFELIX	OCCIDO	RETEXO
AGO	EXEO	INGENS	OMEN	REVERTO
ANIMA	EXITUS	INVENIO	ORBIS	SERPENS
ARDUUS	FATUM	MATRIMONIUM	PASSUS	STUPEO
AUDEO	FAX	MONSTRUM	PLORO	SUPERUS
AURA	FELIX	MUTUS	RECIPIO	UMBRA
AVIDUS	GEMINUS	NUPTA	REGNUM	VANUS

XXXIII. VENTUS ACER – *A BITTER WIND*

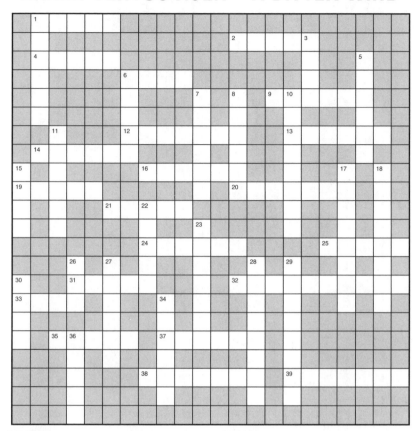

ACROSS

1. I weep, deplore
2. helmet
4. I hope for
6. I swim
9. manliness, courage
12. unhappy
13. I announce, report
14. stag
16. I follow
19. reason, order
20. I call, name
21. trust, faith
24. I tear to pieces, maim
25. nothing
31. I weigh down, burden
32. foreign
33. I go out, depart
35. ground, earth
37. I am born, originate from
38. I grow red
39. shoe

DOWN

1. step
3. bitter, harsh
5. witness
6. ship
7. war
8. right hand
10. innocent, harmless
11. breast, heart
15. tomorrow
17. I conceive
18. cold
22. I grieve
23. iron
26. I do, drive
27. few
28. worse, lower
29. I build, construct
30. mind
34. wind
36. shade, shadow

Select from these words:

ACER	CONCIPIO	FERREUS	LACERO	NUNTIO	RUBESCO
AEDIFICO	CONCURRO	FIDES	MAGIS	OCCIDO	SENECTUS
AGO	CRAS	FRIGIDUS	MENS	PASSUS	SEQUOR
APPELLO	DETERIOR	GALEA	MORDEO	PAUCUS	SPERO
ARDOR	DEXTRA	GRAVO	NASCOR	PECTUS	TESTIS
BELLUM	DOLEO	HUMUS	NATO	PEREGRINUS	UMBRA
CALCEUS	DRACO	INFELIX	NAVIS	PLORO	VENTUS
CERVUS	EXEO	INNOCENS	NIHIL	RATIO	VIRTUS

XXXIV. FIDES INNOCENS – *AN INNOCENT FAITH*

ACROSS

1. mind, spirit
4. breast, heart
5. I snatch apart, tear away
8. despiser
11. burning, heat
13. I tear to pieces, maim
14. fleece, wool
16. innocent, harmless
17. cause
19. I recognize, recall
20. trust, faith
22. tamborine, drum
25. I drive back
26. I end, conclude
27. spear, javelin
28. I grow red

DOWN

2. insane, maddened
3. I suffer pain, grieve
6. foreign
7. I conceal, hide
8. stag
9. booty, prey
10. shade, shadow
12. I swim
15. spread out, scattered
18. I bite
21. suppliant
22. shin bone, pipe, flute
23. wind
24. I weep, wail for

Select from these words:

ANIMUS	DOLEO	INSANUS	PRAEDA	TIBIA
ARDOR	FIDES	LACERO	RECOGNOSCO	TYMPANUM
CAUSA	FINIO	MORDEO	REPELLO	UMBRA
CERVUS	FRONS	NATO	RUBESCO	VATES
CONTEMPTOR	EVENIO	PECTUS	SOLEO	VELLUS
DIRIPIO	HASTA	PEREGRINUS	SUPPLEX	VENTUS
DIVERSUS	INNOCENS	PLORO	TEGO	

XXXV. PRO FORMA – *AS A MATTER OF FORM*

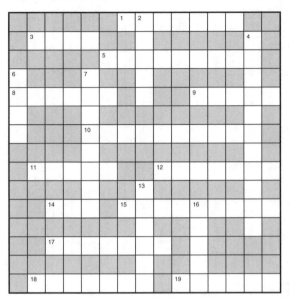

ACROSS

1. to the man, personal (*ad ____*)
3. after the deed is done, retrospective (*ex ____ facto*)
5. in the very act, red-handed (*in ____ delicto*)
8. everywhere, said of allusions found in all parts of a work (____)
9. lesser dog (constellation) (*Canis ____*)
10. a thing already settled (*res ____*)
11. pray for us (*ora pro ____*)
12. so passes away the glory of the world (*sic ____ gloria mundi*)
14. Hail Mary (____ *Maria*)
15. from the beginning (*a ____*)
17. slip of the tongue (*lapsus ____*)
18. temporarily (*pro ____*)
19. in chamber, in private (*in ____*)

DOWN

2. to work is to pray (*laborare est ____*)
4. things to be remembered (____)
6. by that very fact (____ *facto*)
7. wonderful to relate (____ *dictu*)
13. to err is human (____ *humanum est*)
16. for the sake of honor (*honoris ____*)

Select from these words:

ADJUDICATA	HOMINEM	ORARE
AVE	IPSO	PASSIM
BONUS	LABORARE	POST
CAMERA	LINGUAE	PRINCIPIO
CAUSA	MEMORABILIA	TEMPORE
ERRARE	MINOR	TOTO
FLAGRANTE	MIRABILE	TRANSIT
GUSTIBUS	NOBIS	VERITAS

XXXVI. HODIE—CRAS – *TODAY—TOMORROW*

ACROSS

1. I shape, form, invent
3. I obtain, get possession of
8. ram
9. I set free, loosen
13. I scatter, sprinkle
14. I announce, report
15. I bring together, gather
16. I call, name
17. I die, perish
20. faithful
23. I do, make, achieve
24. I drive out
29. I create
30. I die
32. shoe
33. armed
34. fleece

DOWN

2. ship
4. I obtain, get
5. dragon, serpent
6. I retain
7. I hope for
10. I build
11. today
12. I dismiss, let go
15. I go on board, embark
18. business, affair
19. I step out, go out, disembark
21. I pick, choose, select
22. I carry back, take back
25. few
26. oracle
27. I breathe
28. short
31. I join
32. tomorrow

Select from these words:

AEDIFICO	CONSCENDO	FINGO	NEGOTIUM	REFERO
AMITTO	CRAS	GERO	NUNTIO	RETINEO
APPELLO	CREO	HODIE	NUNTIUS	SALVO
ARIES	DELIGO	INDUO	OBTINEO	SCELESTUS
ARMATUS	DRACO	INTEREO	OCCIDO	SPARGO
BREVIS	EGREDIOR	IUNGO	ORACULUM	SPERO
CALCEUS	EXPELLO	MORIOR	PAUCUS	SPIRO
CONFERO	FIDELIS	NAVIS	POTIOR	VELLUS

XXXVII. TIGRIS INGRATUS – *AN UNGRATEFUL TIGER*

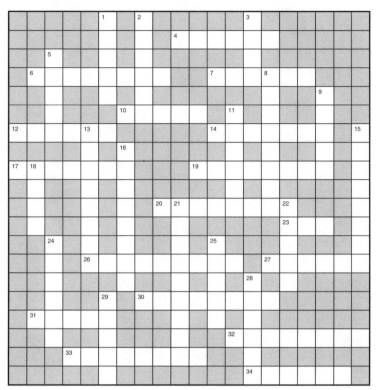

ACROSS

4. I persuade
6. I come to the end of, relieve
7. I am born, originate from
10. I get to know
12. witness
14. sister
17. I fight back
19. I think, reckon, estimate
20. worse, lower
23. art, skill, profession
26. savior (f.)
27. courage, manliness
30. I conceive, imagine
31. madness
32. I prefer, place before
33. I think, judge
34. I follow

DOWN

1. I die, perish
2. I sail
3. mind
5. cloud
8. I bring together, commit
9. I weigh down, burden
11. better
13. unpleasant
15. wicked, evil, nefarious
16. I meet
18. therefore
21. I put out, extinguish
22. reason, order
24. earth, land
25. nothing
28. tiger
29. I approve

Select from these words:

ARBITROR	EXISTIMO	MENS	PEREO	SUADEO
ARS	EXSTINGUO	NASCOR	PRAEPONO	SUBVENIO
COMMITTO	FATEOR	NATA	PROBO	TELLUS
CONCIPIO	FUROR	NAVIGO	RATIO	TESTIS
CONCURRO	GERMANA	NEFARIUS	REPUGNO	TIGRIS
DETERIOR	GRAVO	NIHIL	SALVUS	TIMOR
ERGO	INGRATUS	NOSCO	SEQUOR	VELUM
EXHORTOR	MELIOR	NUBES	SERVATRIX	VIRTUS

XXXVIII. BELLUM HORRENDUM – *A HORRIBLE WAR*

ACROSS

2. ground, earth
4. I turn around, change
7. helmet
9. terrible
10. shout, noise, clamor
12. war
14. drug, medicine
15. I learn
17. I flee, escape from
20. ever-watchful
22. I am left, remain
23. wife
24. more
25. iron
27. in the way, exposed to
28. fixed
29. calm
30. secret
31. heavy

DOWN

1. right hand
2. horrible
3. booty, spoils
5. extinguished
6. I become pale
8. I breathe or blow out
11. I soften, make pliant
13. magic
16. three-formed
18. promise
19. amazing, wonderful
21. cold
26. smoke

Select from these words:

ARDEO	EFFUGIO	HORRENDUS	PALLEO	SUPERSUM
BELLUM	EXSTINCTUS	HUMUS	PERVIGILIS	TERRIBILIS
CADO	FERREUS	MAGICUS	PLACIDUS	TRIFORMIS
CLAMOR	FIXUS	MAGIS	PROMISSUM	UXOR
CONVERTO	FRIGIDUS	MEDICAMEN	RECEDO	
DEXTRA	FUMUS	MIRUS	SECRETUS	
DISCO	GALEA	MOLLIO	SPOLIUM	
EFFLO	GRAVIS	OBVIUS	SUBITO	

XXXIX. BARBA NIGRA – *A BLACK BEARD*

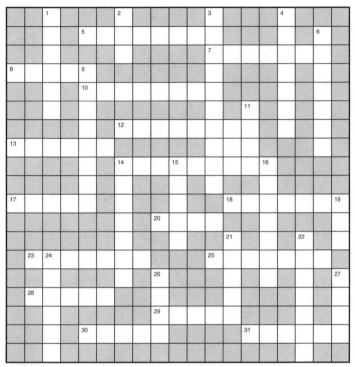

ACROSS

5. heavily, deeply
7. I ascend, go up
8. manner
10. farthest, last
12. I test, try
13. I call again, call back
14. I confess
17. naked
18. money
20. moon
23. length, space
25. strong
28. old
29. olive
30. black
31. chariot

DOWN

1. step, footstep
2. milk
3. I send across, transmit
4. blood
6. I throw, hurl
9. old age
11. therefore
14. hot
15. faithful
16. I regain, take back
19. wing
21. beard
22. I wound
24. respect, piety
26. smell
27. sheep

Select from these words:

ALA	ERGO	LUNA	PECUNIA	TRANSMITTO
ASCENDO	EXPERIOR	MODUS	PIETAS	VALIDUS
BARBA	EXTREMUS	NIGER	RECIPIO	VETUS
CALIDUS	FIDUS	NUDUS	REDDO	VULNERO
CONFITEOR	GRADUS	ODOR	REVOCO	
CONICIO	GRAVITER	OLIVA	SANGUIS	
CURRUS	GUTTUR	OVIS	SENECTUS	
DORMIO	LAC	OVUM	SPATIUM	

XL. RIGOR MORTIS – *RIGOR OF DEATH*

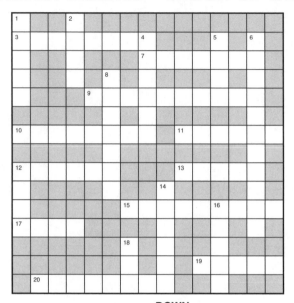

ACROSS

3. at the point of death (*in ____*)
7. off hand, extemporaneous (*ex ____*)
9. inductive reasoning (from effect to cause) (*a ____*)
10. point by point, serially (____)
11. in the same place (____)
12. deductive reasoning (from cause to effect) (*a ____*)
13. about, approximately (____)
15. body of men summoned by sheriff to help keep the peace (*posse ____*)
17. among other things (*inter ____*)
19. righthand page (____)
20. in the highest (*in ____*)

DOWN

1. lefthand page (____)
2. therefore, hence (____)
4. immediately (____)
5. in the place cited (*in ____ citato*)
6. anything needed or desired (____)
8. of the dead (say) nothing but good (*de ____ nil nisi bonum*)
12. distilled water (*aqua ____*)
14. friend of the court (*____ curiae*)
16. one's other self, bosom friend (*____ ego*)
18. things done, deeds (*____ gestae*)

Select from these words:

ALIA	ERGO	PRIORI
ALTER	EXCELSIS	PURA
AMICUS	EXTREMIS	RECTO
BONUM	GUSTIBUS	RES
CIRCA	IBIDEM	SERIATIM
COMITATUS	LOCO	STATIM
DESIDERATUM	MORTUIS	TEMPORE
DICTUM	POSTERIORI	VERSO

XLI. LATRO PUERILIS – *A CHILDISH ROBBER*

ACROSS

4. I terrify, frighten
8. stranger, traveler, pilgrim
9. robber, brigand
10. suitable, fit
11. appropriate
12. the country
14. strip of land
17. I undertake, offer
18. pig, sow
19. I fit, adapt to
20. iron
23. loosened, freed
24. I send away, send down
26. offspring, son
28. bed, couch
29. I depart, go away
31. I offer, present
32. I plow, cultivate

DOWN

1. club, rough stick
2. boyish
3. it is said, handed down
4. tyrant
5. I refuse
6. I kill
7. I set out
8. I persuade
13. public
15. guest, host
16. I put out, display
18. shoe, sandal
21. region, land
22. secure, free from care
23. like, similar
25. I lift up, extol
27. I curve, bend
30. shore, seashore

Select from these words:

APTO	FERREUS	OFFERO	PUERILIS	SUS
APTUS	HOSPES	ORA	RECUSO	SUSCIPIO
ARO	ICTUS	PEREGRINATOR	REGIO	TOLLO
CLAVA	IDONEUS	PERSUADEO	RUS	TERREO
CURVO	ISTHMUS	PINUS	SECURUS	TRADITUR
DEMITTO	LATRO	PROFICISCOR	SIMILIS	TYRANNUS
DISCEDO	LECTUS	PROLES	SOLEA	UTOR
EXPONO	OCCIDO	PUBLICUS	SOLUTUS	VOTUM

XLII. NEFAS CELEBER – *A FAMOUS CRIME*

ACROSS

1. bad deed, crime
3. I praise, honor
5. unaware of, unknown
6. it lies open, is exposed
9. I invite
12. I sacrifice
14. celebrated
16. I kill
17. hospitality
21. barking
23. I make peaceful
24. pleasure, delight
26. death
27. foam, froth
28. goblet, drinking cup
29. sad, gloomy

DOWN

2. I throw down, cast off
4. lying between two seas
6. I beget offspring
7. wicked deed
8. labyrinth
10. I want, wish
11. marriage couch, bedroom
13. banquet, party
15. two-formed
18. applause, clapping
19. cloud
20. powerful
22. I kindle, set on fire
23. paternal
25. white

Select from these words:

ABICIO	FACINUS	LABYRINTHUS	PLAUSUS	VENENUM
ACCENDO	FEROX	LATRATUS	POCULUM	VOLO
ALBUS	FOEDUS	NEBULA	POTENS	VOLUPTAS
BIFORMIS	GENUS	NEFAS	PROCREO	
BIMARIS	HOSPITIUM	NEX	SACRIFICO	
CELEBER	IGNARUS	PACO	SPUMA	
CELEBRO	INTERFICIO	PATET	THALAMUS	
CONVIVIUM	INVITO	PATRIUS	TRISTIS	

XLIII. FORTITUDO PERENNIS – *ETERNAL STRENGTH*

ACROSS

6. scandal, disgrace
9. will, wish
10. I flow back
12. it is necessary
14. abominable, abhorrent
16. I keep, preserve
17. ring
18. nearer
20. I bind, tie
22. strength
24. discordant, inharmonious
26. it is agreeable
27. threshold
28. it is permitted
29. string
30. door
31. it is pleasing

DOWN

1. forehead
2. I decide, determine
3. I submerge, plunge into
4. gliding, falling
5. I unfold, make clear
7. perennial, eternal
8. kindness
11. I build, construct
13. I run, run against
15. I deceive
17. both
19. fatherland
21. work, labor
22. trick, deceit
23. wood
25. box, room, chamber

Select from these words:

AMBO	DIMITTO	IANUA	OPORTET	REFLUO
ANULUS	DISCORS	LAPSUS	OPPROBRIUM	SAEVUS
BENEFICIUM	EVOLVO	LIBET	OPUS	SUBMERGO
CAMERA	FALLACIA	LICET	PATRIA	VOLUNTAS
CONSERVO	FILUM	LIGNUM	PERENNIS	
CONSTITUO	FOEDUS	LIGO	PLACET	
CONSTRUO	FORTITUDO	LIMEN	PROPIUS	
DECIPIO	FRONS	OCCURRO	PUNIO	

XLIV. CANIS SAPIENS – *A WISE DOG*

ACROSS
2. wise
4. buried
6. sow, swine, pig, boar
8. battle
10. I am held, am regarded
12. I do not wish, want
17. law, justice
19. I beg
22. dog
23. deplorable
25. huntress
26. I prefer
28. against

DOWN
1. madness, insanity
3. blood
5. shepherd
7. I force, compel
9. I give birth to
11. exile
13. joy
14. I shake, move, disturb
15. guidance, divination
16. I forget
18. thinking, cogitation
20. liberty
21. sanity, health
24. incense
25. I want, wish
27. citadel

Select from these words:

ARX	FUROR	MALO	SANITAS
AUSPICIUM	HABEOR	NOLO	SAPIENS
CANIS	IMPLORO	OBLIVISCOR	SEPULTUS
COGITATIO	IUS	PARIO	SUS
COGO	IUXTA	PASTOR	TRIBUTUM
COMMOVEO	LAETITIA	PRINCEPS	TUS
CONTRA	LAMENTABILIS	PROELIUM	VENATRIX
EXSILIUM	LIBERTAS	SANGUIS	VOLO

XLV. LAC FRIGIDUM – *COLD MILK*

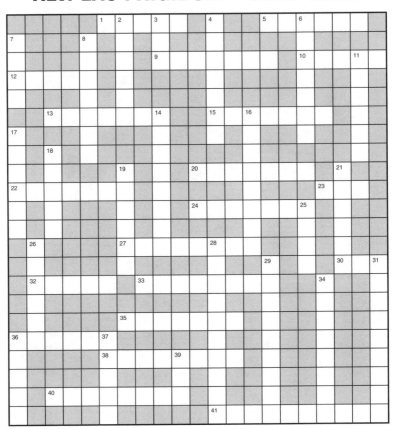

ACROSS

1. robber, brigand
5. I invite
9. health
10. it is permitted
12. beard
13. inharmonious
15. I beg
20. poison
22. I send away, send down
23. milk
24. I throw, hurl
27. exile
30. wing
32. forehead
33. I build
35. I praise, honor
36. against
38. boyish, puerile
40. will, wish
41. scandal, disgrace

DOWN

2. I throw down, cut off
3. countryside
4. sad, gloomy
6. I wound
7. both
8. clapping
11. I display, show
14. old age
16. battle
17. step
18. threshold
19. guest, host
21. box, room, chamber
25. sheep
26. I flow back
28. I kill
29. I confess
31. guidance, divination
34. I test, try
36. dog
37. suitable
39. law, justice

Select from these words:

ABICIO	CELEBRO	EXPERIOR	INVITO	OPPROBRIUM	SANITAS
ALA	CONFITEOR	EXPONO	IUS	OVIS	SENECTUS
AMBO	CONICIO	EXSILIUM	LAC	PERSUADEO	TERREO
APTUS	CONSTRUO	FRONS	LATRO	PLAUSUS	TRISTIS
AUSPICIUM	CONTRA	GRADUS	LICET	PROELIUM	VENENUM
BARBA	CONVIVIUM	HOSPES	LIMEN	PUERILIS	VOLUNTAS
CAMERA	DEMITTO	IMPLORO	NEBULA	REFLUO	VULNERO
CANIS	DISCORS	ITERFICIO	OBLIVISCOR	RUS	

XLVI. RES GESTAE – *THINGS DONE*

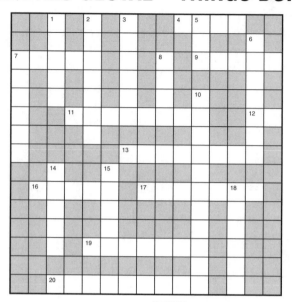

ACROSS

4. with one voice (*una* ___)
7. the order being changed, conversely (*vice* ___)
9. all go out, leave the stage (*exeunt* ___)
11. wonderful to behold (___ *visu*)
12. thou, too, Brutus (*et* ___, *Brute*)
13. there is no disputing about tastes (*de* ___ *non est disputandum*)
16. at equal pace (*pari* ___)
17. I shall please; a harmless substance given as a test in a controlled drug experiment (___)
19. the people rule, Arkansas motto (___ *populi*)
20. out of the depths (*de* ___)

DOWN

1. snake in the grass (*anguis in* ___)
2. so passes away the glory of the world (*sic* ___ *gloria mundi*)
3. divide and rule (*divide et* ___)
5. from the beginning, from the egg (*ab* ___)
6. light and truth, Yale University motto (*lux et* ___)
7. virtue conquers all things (___ *omnia virtus*)
8. I came, I saw, I conquered (*veni, vidi,* ___)
10. the golden mean (*aurea* ___)
14. with a grain of salt (*cum grano* ___)
15. it is sweet and fitting to die for one's country (___ *et decorum est pro patria mori*)
18. life is short, art is long (*vita* ___, *ars longa*)

Select from these words:
BREVIS
DICTUM
DULCE
GUSTIBUS
HERBA
IMPERA
MEDIOCRITAS
MIRABILE
ODIOSA
OMNES
OVO
PASSU
PLACEBO
PROFUNDIS
REGNANT
SALIS
TRANSIT
TU
VACUO
VERITAS
VERSA
VICI
VINCIT
VOCE

XLVII. A NEIGHBORING FOREST – *SILVA VICINA*

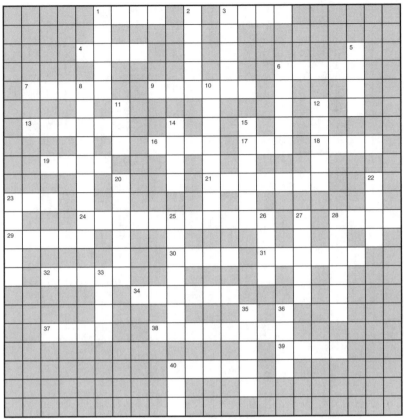

ACROSS

1. verbum
3. oro
4. benignus
6. clamo
7. vox
9. erro
13. agricola
16. pendeo
17. oculus
18. unda
19. voco
21. magister
23. video
24. vicinus
28. ferus
29. exspecto
30. profanus
31. silva
32. campus
34. mater
37. nomen
38. orno
39. habito
40. somnus

DOWN

1. scribo
2. exerceo
3. pronus
5. stella
6. forma
8. querella
10. filia
11. bracchium
12. potentia
14. terra
15. retineo
20. amicus
22. teneo
23. sto
25. suspiro
26. donum
27. equus
28. sapientia
33. vita
35. beatus
36. auxilium
40. filius

Select from these words:

ARM	EVIL	HELP	NEIGHBORING	SON	WILD
AWAIT	EYE	HOLD	POWER	STAND	WISDOM
BREATHE	FARMER	HORSE	PRAY	STAR	WOMAN
CALL	FIELD	KIND	PRONE	TEACH	WORD
CAUSE	FOREST	LAND	RETAIN	TEACHER	WRITE
COMPLAINT	FRIEND	LIFE	SEE	TRAIN	
DAUGHTER	GIFT	LIVE	SHAPE	VOICE	
DECORATE	HANG	MOTHER	SHOUT	WANDER	
DENSE	HAPPY	NAME	SLEEP	WAVE	

XLVIII. A FOREIGN KING – *REX BARBARUS*

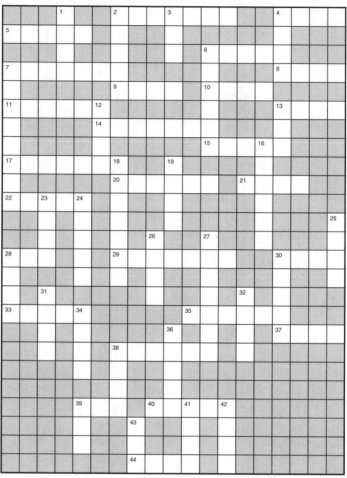

ACROSS
2. fallo
4. libero
5. loquor
6. albus
7. barbarus
8. vivo
9. rex
10. spelunca
11. iniustus
13. mitto
14. repono
15. dubito
17. alius
20. facile
21. durus
22. nox
28. lex
29. vinco
30. canto
33. tertius
35. devoro
37. obtusus
38. prior
39. quaero
40. iacio
44. convenio

DOWN
1. cura
2. bibo
3. finis
4. sentio
6. impius
7. fons
12. verus
13. sedeo
16. ramus
18. gaudeo
19. ignis
23. cresco
24. tabula
25. pagina
26. scio
27. credo
28. sinister
30. gladius
31. piscis
32. iter
34. mortuus
36. tango
38. liber
39. omnis
41. requies
42. ventus
43. gemma

Select from these words:

ALL, ANOTHER, ASK, BEFORE, BELIEVE, BOOK, BRANCH, CARE, CAVE, CONQUER, DEAD, DECEIVE, DEVOUR, DOUBT, DRINK, DULL, EASILY, END, FEEL, FIRE, FISH, FOREIGN, FOUNTAIN, FREE, GEM, GRASS, GROW, HARD, KING, KISS, KNOW, LAW, LEFT, LIVE, MEET, NIGHT, PAGE, REJOICE, REPLACE, REST, ROAD, SEND, SING, SIT, SPEAK, SWORD, TABLE, THIRD, THROW, TOUCH, TRUE, UNJUST, WHITE, WICKED, WIND, YEAR

XLIX. AN AMAZING DRAGON – *DRACO MIRUS*

ACROSS

2. ergo
9. bellum
11. passus
12. finio
13. ploro
14. spolium
16. confero
17. aries
18. aedifico
22. concipio
24. audeo
25. cervus
26. geminus
29. nuntio
30. appello
32. invenio
34. disco
35. arduus
36. mollio
38. placidus
39. occido
40. hasta

DOWN

1. paucus
3. felix
4. ratio
5. fidelis
6. accipio
7. doleo
8. hodie
10. repello
14. acer
15. lacero
18. pectus
19. insanus
20. draco
21. converto
22. frigidus
23. nihil
27. praepono
28. sequor
31. mirus
32. fides
33. uxor
36. fumus
37. navigo

Select from these words:

AMAZING	CONCEIVE	GRIEVE	NOTHING	SMOKE	TODAY
BETTER	DARE	HAPPY	PLACID	SNAKE	TWIN
BITTER	DRAGON	HARD	PREFER	SOFTEN	WAR
BOOTY	END	HEAT	RAM	SPIRIT	WEEP
BREAST	FAITH	HIGHEST	REASON	SPEAR	WIFE
BUILD	FAITHFUL	INSANE	RECEIVE	STAG	
CHANGE	FEW	KILL	REPEL	STEP	
COLD	FIND	LEARN	REPORT	TEAR	
COLLECT	FOLLOW	NAME	SAIL	THEREFORE	

L. A WISE SHEPHERD – *PASTOR SAPIENS*

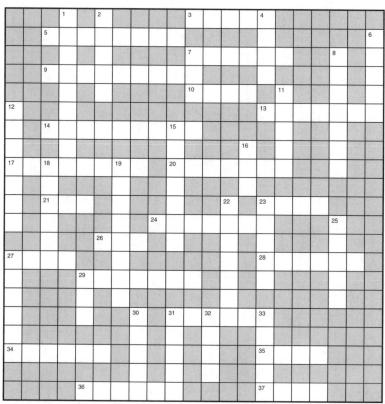

ACROSS

3. conicio
5. pastor
7. puerilis
9. procreo
10. ianua
13. rus
14. construo
17. frons
20. terreo
21. apto
23. ligo
24. decipio
26. tristis
27. gradus
28. latro
29. expono
31. obliviscor
34. poculum
35. ferreus
36. accendo
37. occido

DOWN

1. ergo
2. spatium
4. sapiens
6. convivium
7. lectus
8. ius
11. pecunia
12. confiteor
15. arx
16. sus
18. recuso
19. plausus
22. aptus
23. barba
25. ovis
27. validus
29. canis
30. vulnero
31. cogo
32. genus
33. fallacia

Select from these words:

AGAINST	COUNTRY	FOREHEAD	PERSUADE	SHEEP	WING
APPLAUSE	DECEIVE	FORGET	PIG	SHEPHERD	WISE
BEARD	DISCORDANT	GOBLET	POWERFUL	SPACE	WOUND
BED	DISPLAY	IRON	PREFER	STEP	
BIND	DOG	JUSTICE	PROCREATE	STRONG	
BOYISH	DOOR	KILL	RACE	TERRIFY	
CITADEL	FIT	KINDLE	REFUSE	THEREFORE	
CONFESS	FITTING	MONEY	ROBBER	THROW	
CONSTRUCT	FORCE	PARTY	SAD	TRICK	

ANSWER KEY

I. PRIMA CHARTA Across: 5. specto; 6. charta; 8. paeninsula; 10. insula; 11. amica; 12. desidero; 14. rex; 15. poeta; 17. fugito; 19. primus; 20. amo; 21. porto; 22. habito. **Down:** 1. terra; 2. nova; 3. magnus; 4. timida; 7. transformo; 8. pulchra; 9. ubi; 12. deus; 13. bonus; 16. filia; 17. fabula; 18. narro.

II. AGRICOLA BONUS Across: 3. ubi; 8. specto; 9. longus; 12. magnus; 13. multus; 14. agricola; 19. non; 20. equus; 21. laboro; 23. vita; 25. amo; 26. aqua; 27. silva. **Down:** 1. durus; 2. via; 4. est; 5. servus; 6. porto; 7. fortuna; 10. familia; 11. et; 15. gaudeo; 16. insula; 17. terra; 18. bonus; 19. novus; 22. fama; 24. malus.

III. FEMINA IRATA Across: 1. debeo; 3. laboro; 5. irata; 8. pictura; 9. scribo; 12. magister; 14. doceo; 16. sapientia; 17. temeraria; 20. respondeo; 22. silva; 24. discipuli; 25. lana; 26. nego; 27. clamo. **Down:** 1. dominus; 2. laudo; 4. affirmo; 6. agricola; 7. voco; 10. tempto; 11. formo; 13. experientia; 15. nympha; 18. femina; 19. simulo; 21. nomen; 23. vita.

IV. QUINTA HORA Across: 3. numerus; 7. iniuria; 8. occupo; 10. victoria; 11. dono; 12. monstro; 13. littera; 16. mando; 19. pugna; 20. pecunia; 23. clarus; 25. probo; 26. forma; 27. regina. **Down:** 1. incito; 2. cura; 3. navigo; 4. memoria; 5. quintus; 6. provincia; 9. planus; 14. amicus; 15. hora; 17. nuntio; 18. pugno; 21. nauta; 22. gratus; 23. copia; 24. unda.

V. OCULUS CLARUS Across: 3. filius; 5. pendeo; 7. flamma; 8. prohibeo; 9. oro; 10. donum; 11. multus; 12. sto; 13. beatus; 15. minima; 19. oculus; 20. orno; 21. causa. **Down:** 1. longa; 2. templum; 3. familia; 4. clarus; 5. puer; 6. potentia; 7. fortuna; 14. unus; 15. minor; 16. mala; 17. fama; 18. muto.

VI. TEMPUS FUGIT Across: 3. laude; 5. mortis; 7. toto; 9. libris; 12. generis; 15. populi; 16. firma; 18. res; 19. non. **Down:** 1. quo; 2. utero; 4. emptor; 5. mentis; 6. se; 8. vivendi; 10. culpa; 11. bellum; 13. sapiens; 14. canem; 17. rosa.

VII. LINGUA BARBARA Across: 4. patria; 5. migro; 6. sum; 9. libero; 11. filius; 13. habeo; 15. magister; 17. teneo; 18. captivus; 19. altus; 20. colonus; 23. casa; 25. maneo; 28. barbarus; 29. mereo; 30. doceo; 31. lingua; 32. terreo. **Down:** 1. materia; 2. signum; 3. voco; 7. moveo; 8. vir; 10. gloria; 12. disciplina; 14. annus; 16. socius; 19. animus; 21. semper; 22. video; 24. augeo; 26. habito; 27. puer.

VIII. CAMPUS PLANUS Across: 1. mater; 5. ruina; 7. campus; 10. congelo; 13. ultimus; 16. funera; 17. celeriter; 20. lacrimo; 21. profanus. **Down:** 2. equus; 3. satis; 4. honoro; 6. schola; 8. statua; 9. populus; 10. convoco; 11. querella; 12. exerceo; 14. planus; 15. relinquo; 18. verbum; 19. volo.

IX. CONCORDIA VERA Across: 1. arma; 4. nuntius; 5. exspecto; 7. bellum; 10. officium; 11. causa; 13. terminus; 14. cedo; 15. auxilium; 18. rego; 19. dominus; 21. populus; 23. venio; 24. duco; 25. debeo. **Down:** 2. ago; 3. publicus; 6. concordia; 8. locus; 9. facio; 12. efficio; 15. aequus; 16. maturo; 17. verus; 19. defendo; 20. mitto; 21. pono; 22. latus.

X. EQUUS FERUS Across: 1. campus; 4. suspiro; 7. equus; 8. querella; 10. erro; 13. benignus; 14. magister; 17. voco; 18. agricola; 21. donum; 22. habito; 23. sapientia; 28. auxilium; 29. nomen; 31. oculus; 33. filius; 34. sto; 35. orno; 36. retineo; 39. pendeo; 41. clamo; 42. verbum; 43. terra. **Down:** 2. stella; 3. beatus; 5. potentia; 6. pronus; 9. unda; 10. exspecto; 11. filia; 12. silva; 13. bracchium; 15. scribo; 16. ferus; 19. profanus; 20. vicinus; 24. amicus; 25. narro; 26. exerceo; 27. video; 30. formo; 32. somnus; 37. teneo; 38. mater; 40. oro.

XI. VIR BENIGNUS Across: 2. benignus; 3. fuga; 4. aeternum; 7. celo; 9. devoveo; 11. auxilium; 14. nullus; 15. vir; 16 trans; 20. papyrus; 21. unda; 22. teneo; 23. suspiro. **Down:** 1. ager; 2. bracchium; 3. fugito; 5. maneo; 6. satyrus; 8. densus; 10. miser; 12. umbrosus; 13. sonus; 17. video; 18. erro; 19. puto.

XII. SENTENTIA FIRMA Across: 1. pauci; 5. perpetuus; 8. sententia; 9. firmus; 10. lego; 11. contineo; 14. reliquus; 15. tardus; 16. commodus; 20. incipio; 21. cum; 22. liber; 23. fugio; 24. poeta; 25. traho. **Down:** 2. appello; 3. audio; 4. deus; 6. praesidium; 7. reduco; 12. verbum; 13. varius; 16. convoco; 17. medius; 18. otium; 19. scribo.

XIII. TERRA FIRMA Across: 1. opere; 4. sine; 6. personae; 9. capita; 10. aurora; 12. grata; 13. vobiscum; 16. mortem; 18. avis; 20. quid; 21. infinitum. **Down:** 2. per; 3. de; 5. incognita; 6. paratus; 7. sequitur; 8. novo; 11. amor; 14. meridiem; 15. delicti; 16. magnum; 17. fugit; 18. alma; 19. vidi.

XIV. DELECTAMENTUM! **Across:** *3. victor; 7. verbum; 8. sensa; 9. stella; 12. humanus; 13. invoco; 15. figura; 20. gratus; 22. ferus; 25. vicinus; 26. curo; 27. delectamentum; 29. transporto; 30. somnus.* **Down:** *1. notus; 2. natus; 4. causa; 5. tempus; 6. solus; 10. tendo; 11. pronus; 14. vestimentum; 16. iniuria; 17. appropinquo; 18. neglectus; 19. herbosus; 21. retineo; 23. exspecto; 24. animal; 25. vox; 28. ira.*

XV. MODUS INIMICUS **Across:** *4. obtineo; 6. absum; 8. integer; 9. inimicus; 12. cupio; 13. peto; 14. recipio; 17. beneficium; 20. periculum; 22. inter; 23. conservo; 25. intermitto; 27. primus; 28. remaneo; 30. procedo; 31. natura.* **Down:** *1. sub; 2. retineo; 3. dubito; 5. exemplum; 7. sustineo; 10. moneo; 11. sine; 15. diligentia; 16. porta; 18. egregius; 19. permitto; 20. pro; 21. miser; 24. propono; 26. modus; 29. ego.*

XVI. SENEX IMPIUS **Across:** *2. senex; 5. stagnum; 7. pars; 9. ego; 10. dubito; 11. sacerdos; 13. crater; 15. frondet; 19. miraculum; 21. custos; 23. homo; 24. factus; 25. iustus; 26. praemium; 29. pater; 30. vinum; 31. requies.* **Down:** *1. intro; 2. sedeo; 3. arbor; 4. annus; 6. maiorem; 8. anser; 12. coniunx; 14. rex; 16. verus; 17. prehendeo; 18. piscis; 20. locus; 22. membrum; 24. finis; 25. impius; 27. inter; 28. vivo.*

XVII. MILES PARATUS **Across:** *1. paratus; 4. pes; 5. lex; 6. pax; 10. transporto; 11. miles; 14. fuga; 15. ligo; 18. impedio; 20. factum; 21. ultimus; 22. certus; 24. homo; 25. salus; 26. sto.* **Down:** *2. relinquo; 3. rex; 4. premo; 7. antecedo; 8. provideo; 9. consulo; 12. spatium; 13. tertius; 16. notus; 17. traduco; 19. timidus; 22. clamo; 23. rogo.*

XVIII. RARA AVIS **Across:** *3. memoriam; 4. loco; 8. diem; 9. emerita; 12. profundis; 13. multum; 14. alii; 16. vino; 17. ante; 19. plus; 20. irae; 21. nolo.* **Down:** *1. hoc; 2. sanctorum; 5. operandi; 6. magister; 7. per; 10. ex; 11. pluribus; 14. astra; 15. initio; 18. quod.*

XIX. NOX OBSCURA **Across:** *4. imago; 6. albus; 8. corpus; 9. osculum; 13. spelunca; 14. alter; 17. reporto; 18. medicina; 21. color; 22. mons; 24. obscurus; 25. flumen; 27. caput; 32. laurus; 33. digitus; 35. soror; 36. cresco; 38. virgo; 39. tango; 40. manus; 41. vulnus.* **Down:** *1. facio; 2. ripa; 3. desisto; 5. ars; 6. aqua; 7. amor; 10. contentus; 11. peto; 12. devoro; 14; alius; 15. arcus; 16. dolor; 19. acutus; 20. hostis; 23. iuvenis; 24. obtusus; 26. nox; 28. dico; 29. flor; 30. vigor; 31. musica; 34. folium; 37. ramus; 42. sol.*

XX. ITER FACILE **Across:** *1. caput; 3. pater; 4. vulnus; 5. corpus; 8. celer; 11. hostis; 12. flumen; 13. claudo; 14. tendo; 16. ius; 17. auctoritas; 20. omnis; 23. navis; 24. auctor; 25. virtus; 26. supero.* **Down:** *1. civis; 2. ordo; 3. post; 6. respondeo; 7. tempus; 9. nomen; 10. libertas; 12. fortis; 13. confirmo; 15. facilis; 18. civitas; 19. mons; 21. mare; 22. iter.*

XXI. DOMUS ALBA **Across:** *2. quaero; 5. fallo; 8. mors; 9. dignus; 10. venio; 12. vestigium; 15. relinquo; 16. traho; 18. consilium; 19. parens; 20. bibo; 23. paries; 24. fissum; 26. iter; 27. domus; 28. murmuro.* **Down:** *1. gladius; 3. albus; 4. opto; 5. fugio; 6. sentio; 7. fons; 11. purpureus; 13. recens; 14. prior; 17. herba; 18. convenio; 21. tempus; 22. pomum; 25. leo.*

XXII. DIES DURA **Across:** *1. pomum; 6. libero; 7. vinco; 9. ignus; 11. audio; 13. dies; 14. tertius; 15. hora; 17. res; 18. nomen; 20. domus; 24. sinister; 26. finis; 27. soror; 28. durus; 29. duco; 31. obtusus; 32. rapio; 36. corpus; 37. traho; 38. culpa; 39. quaero; 40. omnis.* **Down:** *2. manus; 3. bibo; 4. arbor; 5. dignus; 8. credo; 10. sedeo; 12. iuvenis; 14. termino; 16. annus; 19. moveo; 21. mortuus; 22. canto; 23. cresco; 25. spelunca; 27. scio; 30. opto; 33. facio; 34. auris; 35. iter.*

XXIII. COR NOBILIS **Across:** *1. spiro; 4. tango; 5. frater; 8. unus; 9. timeo; 10. sedeo; 13. nobilis; 16. cor; 18. mater; 19. nihil; 21. intercipio; 23. alius; 24. hiems; 25. potestas.* **Down:** *1. soror; 2. pars; 3. totus; 6. remitto; 7. curro; 10. solus; 11. communis; 12. expello; 13. neuter; 14. supplicium; 15. incertus; 17. genus; 20. frango; 22. mors.*

XXIV. AD HOC **Across:** *1. compos; 6. tabula; 7. dixit; 8. errare; 10. nauseam; 11. poetica; 14. id; 15. viva; 17. fidelis; 20. canis; 21. absurdum; 22. laude.* **Down:** *2. paterfamilias; 3. vadis; 4. ultima; 5. tu; 9. domini; 11. pares; 12. ex; 13. ave; 16. facie; 18. sum; 19. rata.*

XXV. VICTORIA INCERTA **Across:** *2. nomino; 7. capio; 8. claudo; 10. sono; 12. monumentum; 14. culpa; 17. mitto; 18. audio; 20. urna; 21. scio; 23. durus; 25. moveo; 27. rapio; 28. hora.* **Down:** *1. ignis; 3. incertus; 4. victoria; 5. cura; 6. cornu; 7. cinis; 9. spectator; 11. audacia; 13. mortuus; 14. cursus; 15. lex; 16. corono; 19. damno; 22. culpo; 24. rumor; 26. vinco.*

XXVI. LABOR GRAVIS **Across:** *2. levis; 7. puto; 8. insto; 9. labor; 10. iacio; 14. secundus; 15. ostendo; 17. haereo; 19. mensis; 20. vox; 21. iustus; 24. consisto; 25. vis; 26. alienus.* **Down:** *1. dico; 3. sentio; 4. urbs; 5. opprimo; 6. gravis; 11. contendo; 12. pervenio; 13. munus; 16. prohibeo; 18. acer; 22. scio; 23. solvo.*

XXVII. SECUNDUS AUCTOR Across: *2. pagina; 7. oblique; 8. signus; 9. sententia; 13. tertius; 15. duco; 16. crimen; 17. dies; 19. secreto; 22. auctor; 24. altus; 25. aurum; 27. lavo; 29. heros; 32. forte; 33. omnis; 34. pecco; 35. saxum.* **Down:** *1. invitus; 2. promitto; 3. adversus; 4. damnosus; 5. res; 6. gaudeo; 10. transeo; 11. viridis; 12. facile; 14. secundus; 18. medius; 20. tabula; 21. postis; 23. iacio; 26. credo; 27. liber; 28. venia; 30. curro; 31. simul.*

XXVIII. ORATIO DIFFICILIS Across: *2. summus; 5. ulterior; 8. conditio; 10. extremis; 11. inferior; 12. tribuo; 14. imperium; 15. aptus; 16. dissimilis; 20 gens; 23. conspicio; 26. oratio; 27. iungo; 28. humilis.* **Down:** *1. credo; 3. mille; 4. statuo; 6. proximus; 7. centum; 9. difficilis; 13. opus; 17. similis; 18. iudico; 19. proprius; 21. explico; 22. legatus; 24. instruo; 25. regio.*

XXIX. ARS POETICA Across: *2. pace; 4. vacuo; 6. de; 7. natura; 9. brevis; 11. absentia; 12. bono; 14. cum; 17. vitro; 19. cathedra; 21. amor; 22. esse; 23. spiro.* **Down:** *1. omnia; 2. corpore; 4. verbatim; 5. officio; 8. bene; 10. salutamus; 13. igitur; 15. forma; 16. deo; 18. onus; 20. per; 22. et.*

XXX. AURIS HUMANA Across: *3. reseco; 5. canto; 6. ventus; 8. termino; 10. loquor; 11. gero; 12. lyra; 14. miror; 15. iudicium; 17. auris; 20. inflo; 21. iniustus; 22. iudex; 23. contemno; 24. colo; 25. taceo; 26. barbarus; 27. patior.* **Down:** *1. dexter; 2. libero; 4. decoro; 7. humanus; 9. effodio; 11. gemma; 13. verto; 16. immurmuro; 18. repono; 19. sinister.*

XXXI. PRIMA LUX Across: *5. senatus; 6. super; 7. despicio; 9. exploro; 11. desero; 13. demonstro; 15. exercitus; 17. negotium; 20. princeps; 21. noceo; 22. species; 24. frons; 25. impero; 26. domus.* **Down:** *1. praemitto; 2. ratio; 3. lux; 4. ascendo; 8. intellego; 10. res; 12. reddo; 14. dies; 15. exerceo; 16. supersum; 18. impetus; 19. manus; 23. spes.*

XXXII. SEMPER FELIX Across: *4. ago; 5. retexo; 8. acer; 10. recipio; 13. stupeo; 15. ingens; 16. passus; 18. orbis; 20. monstrum; 22. anima; 23. aura; 26. crudelis; 28. mutus; 29. regnum; 30. accipio; 31. exitus; 32. respicio; 33. geminus.* **Down:** *1. ploro; 2. felix; 3. exeo; 4. audeo; 6. fax; 7. arduus; 9. occido; 11. invenio; 12. reverto; 13. superus; 14. infelix; 17. umbra; 19. fatum; 20. matrimonium; 21. nuptiae; 24. avidus; 25. omen; 27. serpens.*

XXXIII. VENTUS ACER Across: *1. ploro; 2. galea; 4. spero; 6. nato; 9. virtus; 12. infelix; 13. nuntio; 14. cervus; 16. sequor; 19. ratio; 20. appello; 21. fides; 24. lacero; 25. nihil; 31. gravo; 32. peregrinus; 33. exeo; 35. humus; 37. nascor; 38. rubesco; 39. calceus.* **Down:** *1. passus; 3. acer; 5. testis; 6. navis; 7. bellum; 8. dextra; 10. innocens; 11. pectus; 15. cras; 17. concipio; 18. frigidus; 22. doleo; 23. ferreus; 26. ago; 27. paucus; 28. deterior; 29. aedifico; 30. mens; 34.ventus; 36. umbra.*

XXXIV. FIDES INNOCENS Across: *1. animus; 4. pectus; 5. diripio; 8. contemptor; 11. ardor; 13. lacero; 14. vellus; 16. innocens; 17. causa; 19. recognosco; 20. fides; 22. tympanum; 25. repello; 26. finio; 27. hasta; 28. rubesco.* **Down:** *2. insanus; 3. doleo; 6. peregrinus; 7. tego; 8. cervus; 9. praeda; 10. umbra; 12. nato; 15. diversus; 18. mordeo; 21. supplex; 22. tibia; 23. ventus; 24. ploro.*

XXXV. PRO FORMA Across: *1. hominem; 3. post; 5. flagrante; 8. passim; 9. minor; 10. adjudicata; 11. nobis; 12. transit; 14. ave; 15. principio; 17. linguae; 18. tempore; 19. camera.* **Down:** *2. orare; 4. memorabilia; 6. ipso; 7. mirabile; 13. errare; 16. causa.*

XXXVI. HODIE CRAS Across: *1. fingo; 3. potior; 8. aries; 9. salvo; 13. spargo; 14. nuntio; 15. confero; 16. appello; 17. intereo; 20. fidelis; 23. gero; 24. expello; 29. creo; 30. morior; 32. calceus; 33. armatus; 34. vellus.* **Down:** *2. navis; 4. obtineo; 5. draco. 6. retineo; 7. spero; 10. aedifico; 11. hodie; 12. amitto; 15. conscendo; 18. negotium; 19. egredior; 21. deligo; 22. refero; 25. paucus; 26. oraculum; 27. spiro; 28. brevis; 31. iungo; 32. cras.*

XXXVII. TIGRIS INGRATUS Across: *4. suadeo; 6. subvenio; 7. nascor; 10. nosco; 12. testis; 14. germana; 17. repugno; 19. existimo; 20. deterior; 23. ars; 26. servatrix; 27. virtus; 30. concipio; 31. furor; 32. praepono; 33. arbitror; 34. sequor.* **Down:** *1. pereo; 2. navigo; 3. mens; 5. nubes; 8. committo; 9. gravo; 11. melior; 13. ingratus; 15. nefarius; 16. concurro; 18. ergo; 21. exstinguo; 22. ratio; 24. tellus; 25. nihil; 28. tigris; 29. probo.*

XXXVIII. BELLUM HORRENDUM Across: *2. humus; 4. converto; 7. galea; 9. terribilis; 10. clamor; 12. bellum; 14. medicamen; 15. disco; 17. effugio; 20. pervigilis; 22. supersum; 23. uxor; 24. magis; 25. ferreus; 27. obvius; 28. fixus; 29. placidus; 30. secretus; 31. gravis.* **Down:** *1. dextra; 2. horrendus; 3. spolium; 5. exstinctus; 6. palleo; 8. efflo; 11. mollio; 13. magicus; 16. triformis; 18. promissum; 19. mirus; 21. frigidus; 26. fumus.*

XXXIX. BARBA NIGRA Across: *5. graviter; 7. ascendo; 8. modus; 10. extremus; 12. experior; 13. revoco; 14. confiteor; 17. nudus; 18. pecunia; 20. luna; 23. spatium; 25. validus; 28. vetus; 29. oliva; 30. niger; 31. currus.* **Down:** *1. gradus; 2. lac; 3. transmitto; 4. sanguis; 6. conicio; 9. senectus; 11. ergo; 14. calidus; 15. fidus; 16. recipio; 19. ala; 21. barba; 22. vulnero; 24. pietas; 26. odor; 27. ovis.*

XL. RIGOR MORTIS Across: *3. extremis; 7. tempore; 9. posteriori; 10. seriatim; 11. ibidem; 12. priori; 13. circa; 15. comitatus; 17. alia; 19. recto; 20. excelsis.* **Down:** *1. verso; 2. ergo; 4. statim; 5. loco; 6. desideratum; 8. mortuis; 12. pura; 14. amicus; 16. alter; 18. res.*

XLI. LATRO PUERILIS Across: *4. terreo; 8. peregrinator; 9. latro; 10. idoneus; 11. aptus; 12. rus; 14. isthmus; 17. suscipio; 18. sus; 19. apto; 20. ferreus; 23. solutus; 24. demitto; 26. proles; 28. lectus; 29. discedo; 31. offero; 32. aro.* **Down:** *1. clava; 2. puerilis; 3. traditur; 4. tyrannus; 5. recuso; 6. occido; 7. proficiscor; 8. persuadeo; 13. publicus; 15. hospes; 16. expono; 18. solea; 21. regio; 22. securus; 23. similis; 25. tollo; 27. curvo; 30. ora.*

XLII. NEFAS CELEBER Across: *1. facinus; 3. celebro; 5. ignarus; 6. patet; 9. invito; 12. sacrifico; 14. celeber; 16. interficio; 17. hospitium; 21. latratus; 23. paco; 24. voluptas; 26. nex; 27. spuma; 28. poculum; 29. tristis.* **Down:** *1. abicio; 4. bimaris; 6. procreo; 7. nefas; 8. labyrinthus; 10. volo; 11. thalamus; 13. convivium; 15. biformis; 18. plausus; 19. nebula; 20. potens; 22. accendo; 23. patrius; 25. albus.*

XLIII. FORTITUDO PERENNIS Across: *6. opprobrium; 9. voluntas; 10. refluo; 12. oportet; 14. foedus; 16. conservo; 17. anulus; 18. propius; 20. ligo; 22. fortitudo; 24. discors; 26. libet; 27. limen; 28. licet; 29. filum; 30. ianua; 31. placet.* **Down:** *1. frons; 2. constituo; 3. submergo; 4. lapsus; 5. evolvo; 7. perennis; 8. beneficium; 11. construo; 13. occurro; 15. decipio; 17. ambo; 19. patria; 21. opus; 22. fallacia; 23. lignum; 25. camera.*

XLIV. CANIS SAPIENS Across: *2. sapiens; 4. sepultus; 6. sus; 8. proelium; 10. habeor; 12. nolo; 17. ius; 19. imploro; 22. canis; 23. lamentabilis; 25. venatrix; 26. malo; 28. contra.* **Down:** *1. furor; 3. sanguis; 5. pastor; 7. cogo; 9. pario; 11. exsilium; 13. laetitia; 14. commoveo; 15. auspicium; 16. obliviscor; 18. cogitatio; 20. libertas; 21. sanitas; 24. tus; 25. volo; 27. arx.*

XLV. LAC FRIGIDUM Across: *1. latro; 5. invito; 9. sanitas; 10. licet; 12. barba; 13. discors; 15. imploro; 20. venenum; 22. demitto; 23. lac; 24. conicio; 27. exsilium; 30. ala; 32. frons; 33. construo; 35. celebro; 36. contra; 38. puerilis; 40. voluntas; 41. opprobrium.* **Down:** *2. abicio; 3. rus; 4. tristis; 6. vulnero; 7. ambo; 8. plausus; 11. expono; 14. senectus; 16. proelium; 17. gradus; 18. limen; 19. hospes; 21. camera; 25. ovis; 26. refluo; 28. interficio; 29. confiteor; 31. auspicium; 34. experior; 36. canis; 37. aptus; 39. ius.*

XLVI. RES GESTAE Across: *4. voce; 7. versa; 9. omnes; 11. mirabile; 12. tu; 13. gustibus; 16. passu; 17. placebo; 19. regnant; 20. profundis.* **Down:** *1. herba; 2. transit; 3. impera; 5. ovo; 6. veritas; 7. vincit; 8. vici; 10. mediocritas; 14. salis; 15. dulce; 18. brevis.*

XLVII. A NEIGHBORING FOREST Across: *1. word; 3. pray; 4. kind; 6. shout; 7. voice; 9. wander; 13. farmer; 16. hang; 17. eye; 18. wave; 19. call; 21. teacher; 23. see; 24. neighboring; 28. wild; 29. await; 30. evil; 31. forest; 32. field; 34. mother; 37. name; 38. decorate; 39. live; 40. sleep.* **Down:** *1. write; 2. train; 3. prone; 5. star; 6. shape; 8. complaint; 10. daughter; 11. arm; 12. power; 14. land; 15. retain; 20. friend; 22. hold; 23. stand; 25. breathe; 26. gift; 27. horse; 28. wisdom; 33. life; 35. happy; 36. help; 40. son.*

XLVIII. A FOREIGN KING Across: *2. deceive; 4. free; 5. speak; 6. white; 7. foreign; 8. live; 9. king; 10. cave; 11. unjust; 13. send; 14. replace; 15. doubt; 17. another; 20. easily; 21. hard; 22. night; 28. law; 29. conquer; 30. sing; 33. third; 35. devour; 37. dull; 38. before; 39. ask; 40. throw; 44. meet.* **Down:** *1. care; 2. drink; 3. end; 4. feel; 6. wicked; 7. fountain; 12. true; 13. sit; 16. branch; 18. rejoice; 19. fire; 23. grow; 24. table; 25. page; 26. know; 27. believe; 28. left; 30. sword; 31. fish; 32. road; 34. dead; 36. touch; 38. book; 39. all; 41. rest; 42. wind; 43. gem.*

XLIX. AN AMAZING DRAGON Across: *2. therefore; 9. war; 11. step; 12. end; 13. weep; 14. booty; 16. collect; 17. ram; 18. build; 22. conceive; 24. dare; 25. stag; 26. twin; 29. report; 30. name; 32. find; 34. learn; 35. hard; 36. soften; 38. placid; 39. kill; 40. spear.* **Down:** *1. few; 3. happy; 4. reason; 5. faithful; 6. receive; 7. grieve; 8. today; 10. repel; 14. bitter; 15. tear; 18. breast; 19. insane; 20. dragon; 21. change; 22. cold; 23. nothing; 27. prefer; 28. follow; 31. amazing; 32. faith; 33. wife; 36. smoke; 37. sail.*

L. A WISE SHEPHERD Across: *3. throw; 5. shepherd; 7. boyish; 9. procreate; 10. door; 13. country; 14. construct; 17. forehead; 20. terrify; 21. fit; 23. bind; 24. deceive; 26. sad; 27. step; 28. robber; 29. display; 31. forget; 34. goblet; 35. iron; 36. kindle; 37. kill.* **Down:** *1. therefore; 2. space; 4. wise; 6. party; 7. bed; 8. justice; 11. money; 12. confess; 15. citadel; 16. pig; 18. refuse; 19. applause; 22. fitting; 23. beard; 25. sheep; 27. strong; 29. dog; 30. wound; 31. force; 32. race; 33. trick.*

Addenda

Roman Numerals

The following six numerals, variously combined, produce the Roman numerical system.

I	V	X	L	C	D	M
1	5	10	50	100	500	1000

Other numerals are produced in two ways: (1) adding to the basic numeral by placing one or more numerals of equal or smaller value *after* the original numeral;

XI	LV	CX	DLVI	MC
11	55	110	556	1100

or (2) subtracting from the basic numeral by placing one or more numerals *before* the original numeral.

IX	XL	XC	CD	CM
9	40	90	400	900

(The *C* for one hundred is from *centum*, and the *M* for one thousand is from *mille*.)

A smaller numeral between two larger numerals is subtracted from the following numeral:

MCMXC = 1990   CXL = 140

COMMON LATIN ABBREVIATIONS

A.D.   *Anno Domini*—in the year of our Lord

A.M.   *Ante Meridiem*—before noon

P.M.   *Post Meridiem*—after noon

i.e.   *id est*—that is

e.g.   *exempli gratia*—for the sake of an example

ibid.   *ibidem*—in the same place (used often in footnotes to refer to a source just mentioned)

op. cit.   *opere citato*—in the work cited (used often in footnotes to refer to a particular work of an author that has been previously referred to)

sic   *sic*—thus, so (placed in brackets after a quotation to indicate that it is being accurately quoted even though it may seem incorrect or inaccurate)

E PLURIBUS UNUM—One Composed of Many

Like the United States, which has the above motto, nineteen of the states and the District of Columbia have Latin mottoes.

ALABAMA	*Audemus Iura Nostra Defendere*—We Dare Defend Our Rights
ARIZONA	*Ditat Deus*—God Enriches
ARKANSAS	*Regnant Populi*—The People Rule
COLORADO	*Nil sine Numine*—Nothing Without Providence
CONNECTICUT	*Qui Transtulit Sustinet*—He Who Transplanted Still Sustains
IDAHO	*Esto Perpetua*—May She Be Perpetual
KANSAS	*Ad Astra per Aspera*—To the Stars Through Difficulties
MAINE	*Dirigo*—I Direct
MASSACHUSETTS	*Ense Petit Placidam sub Libertate Quietem*—By the Sword She Seeks Peace but Only Under Liberty
MICHIGAN	*Si Quaeris Peninsulam Amoenam Circumspice*—If You Seek a Pleasant Peninsula, Look About You
MISSISSIPPI	*Virtute et Armis*—By Valor and Arms
MISSOURI	*Salus Populi Suprema Lex Esto*—Let the Welfare of the People Be the Supreme Law
NEW MEXICO	*Crescit Eundo*—It Grows as It Goes
NEW YORK	*Excelsior*—Ever Upward
NORTH CAROLINA	*Esse Quam Videri*—To Be Rather than to Seem
OKLAHOMA	*Labor Omnia Vincit*—Labor Conquers All Things
SOUTH CAROLINA	*Dum Spiro Spero*—While I Breathe, I Hope *Animis Opibusque Parati*—Prepared in Mind and Resources
VIRGINIA	*Sic Semper Tyrannis*—Ever Thus to Tyrants
WEST VIRGINIA	*Montani Semper Liberi*—Mountaineers Are Always Freemen
DISTRICT OF COLUMBIA	*Iustitia Omnibus*—Justice to All